INVESTORS IN DEATH

The story of Nunhead Cemetery and the
London Cemetery Company and its successors

by RON WOOLLACOTT

Foreword by Jeff Hart

GW00536591

𝕿𝖍𝖊 𝕱𝖗𝖎𝖊𝖓𝖉𝖘 𝖔𝖋 𝕹𝖚𝖓𝖍𝖊𝖆𝖉 𝕮𝖊𝖒𝖊𝖙𝖊𝖗𝖞

MMX

Front cover : Main entrance to Nunhead Cemetery
(photograph of 1970 by Ron Woollacott)
Back cover: The rear entrance to Nunhead Cemetery 1982
(Author's collection)

First published May 2010 by The Friends of Nunhead Cemetery
c/o 185 Gordon Road
LONDON
SE15 3RT

ISBN 978-0-9539194-8-2

Printed in Great Britain by Catford Print Centre,
LONDON, SE6 2PN

CONTENTS

FOREWORD *by* JEFF HART
Founder and Co-ordinator of Friends of Nunhead Cemetery

Something faintly remarkable has happened in British society over the last thirty years or so. We seem to have come back to terms with death as an everyday occurrence and with cemeteries in particular as places to be valued and visited in a way that seemed to have disappeared after the First World War. It was perhaps, after the huge impact of death and maiming of so many young men that in Britain people started to cross to the other side of the road when passing a cemetery, rather than to follow the Victorian habit of perambulating around the beautifully laid out and maintained grounds where generations of our forebears lay in dignified and peaceful repose. Even the poorest citizen would contribute on a weekly basis to 'burial clubs' to ensure that when their time came a decent burial could be secured.

Today many people have rediscovered the attractions of the vast cemeteries that originated from the early Victorian period. Having slipped into alarming disrepair and neglect after the Second World War, the great privately owned cemeteries were almost literally abandoned, whilst the mid-Victorian municipal cemeteries became subject to increasingly popular 'minimum maintenance' regimes.

In London, the first re-awakenings began with the 'Magnificent Seven' cemeteries of Abney Park, Brompton, Kensal Green, Highgate, Nunhead, Tower Hamlets and West Norwood. Local residents living close to Abney Park Cemetery and then to Highgate Cemetery began to lobby the local powers-that-be to 'do something' about the state of the places that they felt some affinity to, either because they had family buried there, that such neglect was somehow sacrilegious, that they were of architectural or social history value, or that they had become invaluable havens of nature in otherwise heavily urbanised areas. These residents, faced with indifference or hostility, formed themselves into groups, or 'Friends'. In 1981 the third such group, the Friends of Nunhead Cemetery (FONC), came into being. These groups' aims were to improve the condition of the cemeteries and to encourage others to recognise the possibilities of utilising them as places of study and conservation, wildlife preservation or simple peaceful recreation. From this start, the 'Cemetery Friends Movement' has spread to all parts of the country and there are now more than seventy such groups that are members of the National Federation of

Cemetery Friends. In some cases they have worked constructively with enlightened cemetery owners to improve maintenance and facilities for visitors to graves or the studious or casual visitor intent on enjoying all that such sites now have to offer. In other cases there have been bitter legal battles to prevent the wholesale destruction of monuments and buildings by philistine owners. Whether raising money at jumble sales, leading tours of their cemeteries, publishing books, establishing 'cemetery trails' or political lobbying, these stalwart volunteers have contributed to opening the eyes of both the British public and the 'authorities' to the now undoubted amenity and cultural value of our cemeteries. That influence has now spread abroad with the formation of the Association of Significant Cemeteries in Europe.

But how did this marvellous legacy come down to us today? Who and how was it decided that burial grounds not associated with churches should be permitted to bury the dead and charge huge sums for the privilege? How did the London Cemetery Company come to own and operate both the Nunhead and Highgate cemeteries - two jewels of the cemetery world - attract its customers and make its money? Here you will find the highs and lows, and the sometimes moving and amusing moments of its history. Today, the cemetery movement and the wider history of the interment of the dead and funerary customs are the subject of many scholarly works, but none will have been researched and written with the single-minded care and dedication shown by author Ron Woollacott, a local historian, who pursued the solitary task of recording the lives and works of the many persons interred at Nunhead Cemetery, until being supported, as the first and only Chairman of the Friends of Nunhead Cemetery, by many volunteers interested in the various aspects of interest the cemetery now has to offer. This book is as much a testimony to Ron - recently appointed MBE - as it is to the founders and employees of the London Cemetery Company.

I urge you now to read on and appreciate the efforts that have bequeathed to us, and generations to come, the pleasure that All Saints Cemetery, Nunhead, has to offer today as much as for the solace and comfort - and, indeed, pleasure - it offered to generations past.

Thank you Ron, and to all members of FONC, and to you the reader for caring about Nunhead Cemetery.

Jeff Hart
FONC Co-ordinator
April 2010

PREFACE & ACKNOWLEDGEMENTS

Nunhead Cemetery has always been special to me, not only because my dear grandparents and three generations of my wife's family are buried there dating back to 1897, but quite simply because it is such a remarkable place. I grew up just a few streets away, and resided most of the last 70-odd years as close as a few yards, and no more than a couple of miles, from the cemetery gates.

Living in Linden Grove, practically opposite the main entrance to Nunhead Cemetery for 18 years (from 1958 to 1976), I had ample time to explore the miles of winding roads, secret pathways, hidden tombs and shadowy corners, long before the private owners abandoned the cemetery in the spring of 1969. Happily, the cemetery is now a Grade II* listed historic landscape and its future is assured.

I am grateful to Mr Bob Smyth, founder and first Chairman of the Peckham Society and the author of *City Wildspace* and *The Green Guide to Urban Wildlife,* for having persuaded me to write a short piece on Nunhead Cemetery for the society's newsletter back in 1975, and to Professor Emeritus James Stevens Curl, the country's foremost authority on Victorian cemeteries, funerary art and architecture, for unwittingly encouraging me to discover more about the development of 19th century cemeteries. Indeed, it was Professor Curl's book, *The Victorian Celebration of Death,* first published in 1972, that inspired me to delve deeper into the history and origins of Nunhead Cemetery, its proprietors, employees, and the people buried there.

Professor Curl's authoritative paper, *Nunhead Cemetery - A History of the Planning, Architecture, Landscaping and Fortunes of a Great Nineteenth-Century Cemetery,* published in the Transactions of the Ancient Monuments Society in 1977, and his excellent book, *The Victorian Celebration of Death* (a new edition was published in 2000), are essential reading for anyone wishing to study the fascinating history of the 19th century cemetery movement.

I am also indebted to the former Superintendents of Southwark Council's Cemeteries Department, namely the late Mr Lou Hedger, Mr Jeff Webber and Mr Terry Connor, for allowing me to 'bury' myself deep in the cemetery records on numerous occasions over many years. I am also grateful to all the staff based at Camberwell New Cemetery for their kindness and hospitality, in particular Messrs Chris Barr, Tony Black, Michael Buckley, Bert Evans, Michael O'Shaughnessy and Fred Wilson.

I must thank Mr Anthony Wragg, former Deputy Borough Engineer and Surveyor of Southwark Council, for providing me with much useful information concerning the Council's acquisition of the cemetery, and Mr Frank Zobel, Mrs Ann Baker and Ms Julie Ferguson of New Zealand, for supplying information about their interesting ancestors: George Gillingham, James Clements and Robert Forster, all three of whom were long serving employees of the London Cemetery Company, and to the late Mrs Ethel Brackley, my next-door neighbour in Linden Grove, whose husband, Mr Ernest Brackley, was for so many years the uniformed gatekeeper at Nunhead Cemetery. Thanks also to Mrs Jean Brown, Mrs Rosemary Gill, Mr Stan Hyam and Mr Steve Wright, for information and photographs.

I should also like to extend my thanks to the staff of Nunhead Library; Southwark Local Studies Library; Westminster Reference Library, Buckingham Palace Road; and the Library of the Society of Genealogists, for their assistance when I was carrying out much of my research back in the 1970s and 1980s.

My thanks to all past and present members of the General Committee of the Friends of Nunhead Cemetery (FONC) for their support, in particular Mr Chris Knowles and Ms Mary Anne Bonney, both enthusiastic founder members of FONC, who served as Vice-Chairman and Secretary respectively during the group's early years, and Ms Gwyneth Stokes, long-serving FONC Committee Member and Secretary of the National Federation of Cemetery Friends, for her helpful advice and for casting an expert eye over my typescripts.

My special thanks to my wife Maureen and her sister, Miss Linda Martin, my two daughters, Mrs Michèle Louise Burford and Mrs Simone Whipp, and my dear mother-in-law, Mrs Sybil Vearonelly, who was born in a house just a few yards away from Nunhead Cemetery almost a century ago in 1912. All five of whom have been keen supporters of FONC since its inception in 1981.

Last but not least I should like to thank Mr Jeff Hart, the founder and Co-ordinator of FONC, for writing the foreword to this book. It was his foresight, determination, dedication and enthusiasm, that helped save the beautiful and historic Victorian cemetery at Nunhead, for everyone to appreciate and enjoy - both now and in the future.

Ron Woollacott
Nunhead, 1975 - 2010

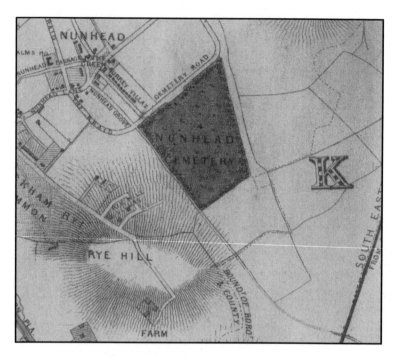

Nunhead Cemetery in 1856
surrounded by farms, fields and market gardens.

Picture Credits

Acknowledgement is made to the following persons for their kind permission to reproduce photographs: Ann Baker page 79; Jean Brown page 73; Peter Eliot of Australia page 26; Rosemary Gill page 33; Stan Hyam pages 70, 81; Steve Wright page 86; Frank Zobel pages 29, 47, 68, 71

Photographs by the author: front cover, pages 22, 42, 45, 48, 52, 54, 60, 88, 91, 116

Author's collection: pages 10, 17, 20, 21, 30, 64, 65, 80, 84, 96, 103, back cover

FONC's collection: pages 100, 102

1: HISTORICAL BACKGROUND

The story of Nunhead Cemetery begins with the movement to establish safe, secure, and sanitary burial grounds outside the heavily built up and densely populated areas of central London.

In the early years of the 19th century, London's dead were buried in churches and churchyards and Nonconformist graveyards in and around the cities of London and Westminster. The Mortuary Returns of the Parish Clerks of London, which cover the years 1741 to 1837, although incomplete, give the number of dead buried in central London's overflowing graveyards in the same period as in excess of 2.1 million.[1] Few deceased persons were allowed to rest in peace, however, as most graveyards had been in use for centuries and, as a consequence, the dead were regularly unearthed to make room for others. The mortal remains of the eminent and wealthy were generally laid to rest in burial vaults within their parish churches where they were less likely to be disturbed.

There were numerous reports of human remains littering the overcrowded graveyards, and the spread of disease was often linked with these miserable places of decaying mortality. Indeed, there was little respect for the dead and even less for the living whose dwellings adjoined the unsavoury burial grounds. Furthermore, few freshly buried cadavers were safe from the evil clutches of the resurrectionists (body-snatchers) who plundered unprotected burial grounds and made a grim living by selling the recently deceased to surgeons and anatomists for medical research.[2]

Mrs Holmes, the author of *The London Burial Grounds* published in 1896, claimed that for every single body removed from the graveyards by body-snatchers, over 100 more were removed simply to make room for others.

Private and promiscuous burying places

The overcrowded graveyards encouraged unscrupulous individuals, intent on making easy money, to open private burying places which were no better, and often worse, than the graveyards they sought to replace.

By 1836, in which year the London Cemetery Company Act authorising the establishment of the Nunhead and Highgate cemeteries received Royal Assent, over a dozen privately owned burying places were operating in and around London, one of which, Messrs Hoole and Martin's speculation known as 'New Bunhill Fields', had been established at

Deverell Street, near the Old Kent Road, in 1820. By 1838 more than 10,000 bodies had been crammed into just one acre of ground. The cellar beneath a small chapel in the centre of the ground was used for 'temporary' burial and, for the sum of 20 shillings (£1), a corpse could be deposited 'on lease', no questions asked, for six months. Thomas Jenner, a patten maker, who lived nearby at 7 Dover Place West, was paid £20 per year to officiate at funerals dressed as a minister of religion.[3]

Enon Chapel, another speculation, was established in 1823 by the Reverend Mr Howse, a Dissenting minister, whom it would seem was more interested in making money than in saving souls. The chapel, in Clement's Lane, Strand, was built without a burial ground attached and, as a consequence, many hundreds of bodies were piled into pits dug beneath its floor. It was also claimed that bodies were dumped into the sewer that ran under the cellar, and discarded coffins were used as firewood by the reverend gentleman. By 1842 the cellar contained around 11,000 corpses in a space less than 60 feet by 30 feet and just six feet deep.[4]

Several undertakers operated burial grounds. Butler's burial ground, at Horsleydown in the Parish of St Olave's, Southwark, was simply a few backyards behind occupied houses when it opened for burials in 1822. The grave spaces were quickly used up, and so the enterprising undertaker, intent on making even more money, acquired the cellars beneath four houses adjoining the burial ground and filled them with coffins. The cellars were still in existence when Mrs Holmes, who described such burying places as 'private and promiscuous', carried out her extensive survey of London's burial grounds in the 1890s.

The setting up of the joint-stock cemetery companies

The reluctance of the authorities, both ecclesiastical and civil, to deal with the growing menace of the overcrowded graveyards, gave rise to the formation of the joint-stock cemetery companies. At first, the Established Church was against the setting-up of profit-making commercial cemeteries, indeed, the Bishop of London opposed in Parliament the Bill for the formation of a commercial cemetery for London, and one of his archdeacons published a pamphlet claiming that London's churchyards were 'perfectly healthy' and not at all as offensive as claimed by the promoters of the new commercial cemetery companies.[5]

The capital's first commercial cemetery was established by the General Cemetery Company at Kensal Green, Middlesex,[6] despite the obstacles put in the way of the promoters by those persons determined to keep up the 'horrid practices of the old London system' of interments. George Frederick Carden (1798-1874), a barrister-at-law, was the man behind the General Cemetery Company.[7] Carden started his long and vigorous campaign for a cemetery for London as early as 1824. The General Cemetery Company was eventually incorporated by a private Act of Parliament in the summer of 1832, and the greater part of Kensal Green Cemetery was consecrated by the Bishop of London on the 24th January 1833.[8]

To appease the Church authorities, and to compensate the clergy for loss of revenue, the General Cemetery Company was obliged to pay a fee to the incumbent of the parish from which each body was brought for burial if the parish was within the Bills of Mortality and the Diocese of London. A fee of five shillings (25p) was payable for burials in catacombs, vaults and brick-graves, and one shilling and sixpence (7½p) was payable for each body interred in consecrated ground.[9]

Despite this unfair financial burden imposed on the General Cemetery Company by Act of Parliament, Kensal Green Cemetery flourished, and this led to the formation of several more joint-stock cemetery companies. Between 1837 and 1841 a further six commercial cemeteries were laid out in a ring around the capital.

In contrast to the sordid private burying places such as the New Bunhill Fields and the Enon Chapel, which were set up first and foremost as money-making concerns, the new commercial cemeteries were created and managed by enterprising professional gentlemen and others who were anxious to provide decent, secure, spacious, and above all hygienic, though nevertheless profitable, burial grounds outside the densely populated areas of central London.

The new cemeteries, set in pleasant semi-rural surroundings, were not simply places to lay the deceased to rest, but were also intended for the 'spiritual improvement of visitors'. The original reasons of decency and sanitation had given way to transforming the cemeteries into a 'cultural institution for the living',[10] where people could come and meditate as well as pay their respects to the dead and admire the monuments.

The campaign for public cemeteries

Interment in the commercial cemeteries was expensive and, as a consequence, only the wealthy could afford to purchase burial rights. A few inexpensive common (communal) plots were set aside for the less well-

13

off in most commercial cemeteries, nevertheless, London's poorest citizens were not generally well catered for.[11]

Notwithstanding the success of the commercial cemeteries - by 1840 over 4,000 interments had taken place at Kensal Green alone - burials in the capital's graveyards continued as before, and it soon became clear that urgent action was necessary if the problems of the overcrowded churchyards, cramped and overflowing Nonconformist burial grounds, and the insanitary private burying places such as New Bunhill Fields and the Enon Chapel were to be resolved.[12]

George Alfred Walker (1807-84), a zealous burial reformer, who was by profession a surgeon at 101 Drury Lane, and the proprietor of a bath house, led a campaign for the closure of all burying grounds in the built-up areas of London and, in 1840 he presented 'damning' evidence before a Select Committee at the House of Commons. Regrettably, his evidence was 'coolly received' and 'little appreciated' at the time.

The indomitable Walker, however, who was neither deterred nor discouraged by the Select Committee's failure to take his evidence seriously, later drew up a petition for the removal of all human remains from populous places which he presented to Parliament in 1842. In 1847 he gained access to the Enon Chapel and removed, at his own expense, 'four upheaved vanloads' from the cellar of the chapel and 'the whole mass of bodies' was buried in one huge pit in Norwood Cemetery.[13]

Another ardent cemetery campaigner, the architect and landscape gardener, John Claudius Loudon (1783-1843), whose interest in the formation of extramural public cemeteries began in the 1820s, suggested laying out several cemeteries in a ring around London in the style of botanical gardens. Loudon was the main protagonist in the garden cemetery movement and his ideas influenced cemetery design.[14]

By the mid-1840s the campaign to abolish intramural burials was well under way. The Liberal MP, William Alexander Mackinnon (1789-1870), had introduced a Bill prohibiting burials in urban areas, and the public health reformer, Edwin [later Sir Edwin] Chadwick (1800-90), had produced his famous report advocating the closure of all burial grounds in London and the provision of public cemeteries for the poor. He also proposed the compulsory acquisition of the commercial cemeteries. Sir Richard Broun (1801-58) 'a great promoter of extramural burial' proposed the construction of a huge necropolis at Woking in Surrey to receive London's dead, and by 1849 the Society for the Abolition of Burials in Cities and Towns had been formed and the campaigning surgeon, George Alfred

Walker, was President. Immediate legislation to ban intramural burial was being demanded, and in 1850 the first of several prohibitory acts, the Metropolitan Interments Act, was passed.[15] Among its powers, the Act gave Edwin Chadwick's newly created, though short-lived General Board of Health, the power to compulsorily purchase all the commercial cemeteries in the Metropolitan area. The first two cemeteries ear-marked for acquisition were Brompton and Nunhead. Following the abolition of the General Board of Health in 1852, however, only Brompton Cemetery was acquired under the Act.

The London Cemetery Company

Nunhead Cemetery was established in 1840 by the London Cemetery Company which had opened its first cemetery at Highgate in 1839. It was the sixth and, at 52 acres in extent, the largest of the seven great commercial cemeteries created around London between 1832 and 1841.

The London Cemetery Company, a once prosperous but now defunct cemetery company, was founded by Stephen Geary (1797-1854), entrepreneur, architect and surveyor, of 10 Hamilton Place, King's Cross. Geary's earlier projects included a theatre, which was never completed, a collegiate school, and a curious octagonal building erected at Battle Bridge, Middlesex. The latter, originally a police station and later a public house, was surmounted by an 'absurd' statue of King George IV which stood around 60 feet high. The statue was removed in 1842, and the entire structure, which gave its name to King's Cross, was eventually demolished in 1845.[16]

The London Cemetery Act of 1836 empowered Geary's company to create three cemeteries, not exceeding a total of 150 acres, 'Northward, Southward, and Eastward, of the Metropolis.' The capital of the Company was limited to £100,000 consisting of 5,000 shares at £20 each.[17]

George Collison, a promoter of the rival Abney Park Cemetery Company in north London, complained that the London Cemetery Company Act, which authorised a company to build more than one cemetery in the Metropolitan area, was 'a very sorry piece of legislation creating a monopoly of cemetery interment in favour of the one company,'[18]

The newly incorporated London Cemetery Company opened an office at 22 Moorgate Street in the City of London. Richard Cuttill (c.1797-1862) was appointed Managing Director, and Charles Burls (1814-1896) of the Red House, Peckham Rye, was appointed Head Clerk and served as

Secretary and Registrar from 1843 to 1846.

The London Cemetery Company, in common with the General Cemetery Company, was liable to pay fees to the clergy of the parishes from which each body originated, but in the case of the London Cemetery Company the Church had obtained better terms. For example, the General Cemetery Company was liable to pay fees only to the incumbents of parishes within the Bills of Mortality and Diocese of London, whereas the London Cemetery Company was obliged to pay a fee to the incumbents of *all parishes* within a five mile radius of any cemetery the company might establish. The fees, however, were the same as those imposed at Kensal Green i.e. five shillings (25p) for burials in catacombs, vaults and brick-graves and one shilling and sixpence (7½p) for each body interred in a common or private earth grave in consecrated ground. The Bishop of London claimed his clergymen were once again 'great losers'. He bemoaned the fact that he was indisposed when the London Cemetery Company Act was passed and was not, therefore, in a position to ensure even better terms of compensation were obtained. The West of London and Westminster Cemetery, founded at Brompton the same year as Nunhead, was obliged to pay 10 shillings (50p) to the clergy from whose parish each corpse originated. The Bishop thought those fees were fairer.

The London Cemetery Company's proprietors

The proprietors (shareholders) of the London Cemetery Company were drawn from all walks of life, including the Established and Nonconformist churches, the aristocracy, the gentry, the military, the legal and medical professions, accountants, politicians, civil engineers, manufacturers, merchants, shopkeepers, stockbrokers, stonemasons, tradesmen, undertakers, and anyone else for that matter, who could afford the purchase price of the shares.

Benjamin Edgington (1794-1869), a marquee maker by appointment to HM Queen Victoria, was a large shareholder and a regular attendant at the General Meetings of Proprietors until his death, though he never once served on the Board. He died at his residence, 'The Elms', Tooting, leaving a personal fortune of £120,000, and was buried at Nunhead.

David Cripps Preston JP (1842-1925), a monumental mason and sculptor with workshops near Nunhead Cemetery, was another large shareholder. A regular and vociferous attendant at the General Meetings from 1892 until 1915, he never sought election to the Board. Preston's name disappears from the Company's Minute Books after July 1915. He took an active role in local affairs and served as a Camberwell Vestryman and local magistrate. He died at his Dulwich residence in 1925, aged 83, and was buried in the Dissenters' ground at Nunhead.

In the early years the proprietors met at Radley's Hotel, 10 New Bridge Street, Blackfriars, or at the Salisbury or Anderton's hotels in Fleet Street. For 70 years, between 1878 and 1948, the General Meetings took place at the Company's Head Office in the City. After 1948 the shareholders met at Nunhead Cemetery where the Company's Head Office had been based since the Second World War. In the 1950s several meetings were held at the offices of Smallfield, Rawlins and Co, Chartered Accountants, and St Bride's Institute in the City of London.

Directors and auditors elected at General Meetings

The directors were elected at the General Meetings of Proprietors to serve a period of three years, and were eligible to stand for re-election to the Board on completion of their term of office. Dr John Hue, a physician and surgeon, was a director for 38 consecutive years, and Herbert Hardwick Trist, a wine merchant, served on the Board for over half a century.

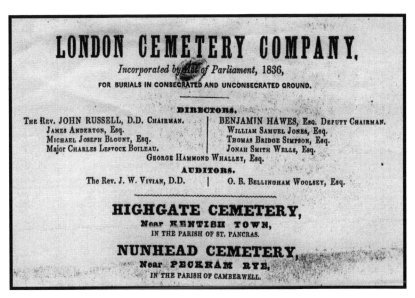

London Cemetery Company letterhead c.1848

In the 1860s the directors received a remuneration of £200 per annum tax paid. Their salary was raised to £300 in 1865, £400 in 1895, and £500 in 1900. In 1919 their pay was fixed at £800 per annum, and by 1948 they each received £1,430 less income tax.

The Board originally consisted of ten directors. In 1905 this number was reduced to eight and in 1917 to seven. By 1960 the Board was made up of just two directors, one of whom was the Chairman and the other the Company Secretary.

A number of distinguished gentlemen served on the Board over the years including the Revd Dr John Russell (1787-1863), a former headmaster of Charterhouse School; Sir Benjamin Hawes MP (1797-1862); George Hammond Whalley MP (1813-1878); Horace Hutchinson (1859-1932), a well-known golfer, all-round sportsman and author; James Anderton (1752-1868), lawyer and Common Councillor in the City of London; Stephen, Baron de Gurbs (1800-1892); Captain James Combes Giffard (1821-1884), late Madras Army; the Revd Dr James William Vivian (1785-1876), Rector of St Peter-le-Poer; General William Nelson Hutchinson (1803-1895), late Grenadier Guards; Major General William Taylor Corrie (1838-1931); George Robert Bengough (1806-1888), who was also Chairman of the General Cemetery Company from 1879 to 1882; and James Richard Neville Stopford, 7th Earl of Courtown (1877-1957).

Two auditors were elected at the General Meetings and were eligible to stand for re-election at the conclusion of their term of office. Frank Steane Price, chartered accountant, and a partner in the firm of Price, Waterhouse and Co, served as auditor for 30 consecutive years eventually resigning in 1947.

In 1868 the auditors each received a fee of 10 guineas (£10.50). In 1923 the auditors' fee was raised to 25 guineas (£26.25), and in 1951 it was doubled to 50 guineas (£52.50).

The accounts were presented annually, but following the Buxton fraud (see chapter 3), half-yearly accounts were produced. General Meetings were held twice a year between 1865 and 1920, and annually from 1921 to 1960 inclusive. Occasional Special Meetings were convened when deemed necessary.

Several eminent gentlemen served as auditor including Bryan Donkin (1835-1902), civil engineer and grandson of Bryan Donkin FRS; Sir Arthur Lowes Dickinson (1859-1935), chartered accountant; and Sir Walter Edmund Parker CBE (1908-1981), chartered accountant.

The Company's first cemetery is laid out at Highgate

Approximately 20 acres were acquired for the London Cemetery Company's Northern Station (the Company referred to its cemeteries north and south of the river as stations) near Kentish Town in the Parish of St Pancras, Middlesex. The site, on the southern slopes of Highgate Hill, was purchased from the Cave family for the sum of £3,500, and once formed part of the grounds of Ashurst House, a large mansion belonging to Sir William Ashurst (1647-1720), a former Lord Mayor of London, and was afterwards the seat of Sir Alan Chambre (1739-1823). The mansion later housed a school for young gentlemen before being demolished in 1830 to make way for St Michael's Church in 1832.[19]

Stephen Geary's original plans for the Northern Station incorporated St Michael's Church with an entrance from the church grounds into the top of the cemetery. A Nonconformist chapel, with burial vaults beneath, was planned for the centre of the cemetery, and this was to be connected by a tunnel leading to an entrance at the foot of the hill. This particular plan, which included a terrace with catacombs and ornamental lake, appears to have been abandoned in favour of the present layout.[20]

David Ramsay of the Stanhope Nurseries in Brompton, who had carried out landscape work at Kensal Green Cemetery, was appointed landscape gardener and, in association with Geary, created a picturesque landscape with winding roads, plantations and flower beds. Two chapels were constructed in the Gothic style 'bristled all over with pinnacles', one for Anglicans and the other for Dissenters, alongside 'a grand Tudor gateway' in Swain's Lane. A second entrance was constructed adjoining St Michael's Church but, as it was not sanctioned by the Church authorities, it was kept permanently closed by order of the Bishop of London. Burial vaults and catacombs were constructed including a sunken avenue leading to a ring of tombs surrounding a Cedar of Lebanon forming 'a mass of building in the Egyptian style of architecture.'[21]

Highgate Cemetery opens for burials

On Monday 20th May 1839, the Company's Northern Station, or Highgate Cemetery as it became known, was consecrated and dedicated to St James by the Lord Bishop of London. A few acres were left unconsecrated for the burial of Dissenters in accordance with the London Cemetery Company Act. The first body to be interred was that of Elizabeth

Highgate Cemetery c.1842

Jackson of Golden Square, Holborn, whose burial took place three days after the consecration, and a further 203 interments had taken place before the year was out.[22]

Highgate Cemetery was not built without opposition. The local residents were angry at first and petitioned against the construction of a cemetery in their neighbourhood; however, when they saw the beautifully landscaped grounds, hilly paths and ornamental planting, applications were made to purchase keys which enabled them to gain access to the cemetery and visit the grounds whenever they desired.[23]

An anonymous admirer described a visit to Highgate Cemetery in 1839 as follows:

Throughout the grounds, parterres of sweet-scented flowers, picturesque trees, and clumps of evergreens are scattered in the most appropriate spots. As we ascend the hill we see on the left an archway of Egyptian character, which forms the entrance to the catacombs, in which the coffins are placed in cavities formed by the most solid masonry. Having examined these, a circular path brings us again to the entrance. On the top of the central compartment of catacombs is a fine cypress-tree, spread-

20

ing its dark branches over the whole. Leaving the catacombs, we find ourselves almost immediately on a broad level terrace, with a handsome balustrade at the very foot of the church (St Michael's). The view from this point is remarkably fine, and is alone well worth a visit from the metropolis. The beauties of the place, indeed, appear to be fully appreciated, for the gardens as we may not inappropriately term the grounds, are daily filled with persons, evidently enjoying the quiet, the pure air, and the splendid landscape.[24]

A view inside Highgate Cemetery c.1873

George Collison, Secretary of the Abney Park Cemetery Company, was not impressed. Having carefully considered 'all the aspects of Highgate Cemetery and its surroundings' he came to the conclusion that it was 'greatly inferior' to the cemeteries at Kensal Green and Norwood. 'One is so much accustomed to associate ideas of pleasure and holiday making with Highgate and its beautiful vicinity,' he complained, 'that a cemetery seems almost the last place we should think of meeting with there.' He went on to describe the architecture as 'extravagant and unsuitable' and complained about the 'picnic parties' he had witnessed taking place in the consecrated ground.[25]

In 1839, James Bunstone Bunning (1802-63) of 34 Great Guildford Street, London, succeeded Stephen Geary as architect and surveyor to the London Cemetery Company. A former district surveyor to the Parish of Bethnal Green and surveyor to the Foundling Hospital Estates, he had worked with Geary on the layout of Highgate Cemetery and was responsible for some of its buildings. Professor James Stevens Curl attributes the design of the Egyptian Avenue to him.[26]

The Terrace Catacombs in Highgate's West Cemetery 1982

2: NUNHEAD CEMETERY

The success of Highgate Cemetery encouraged the directors to proceed without delay with their Southern Station. The site chosen was Nunhead Hill, near Peckham Rye, in the Parish of St Giles, Camberwell, Surrey. It bordered the Parishes of St Paul, Deptford and Lewisham, in the county of Kent.

Nunhead Hill rises steeply to 200 feet above sea level and afforded panoramic views over central London, Surrey and Kent. It was a favourite haunt of artists and poets and the perfect setting for a romantic cemetery. Indeed, it was the rural retreat that Robert Browning, the poet, had visited with his father as a child, and where his contemporary, the artist and visionary Samuel Palmer, sought inspiration before finding his 'Valley of Vision' at Shoreham in Kent. Palmer returned to the hallowed hill in 1848 to bury both his beloved infant daughter Mary, and his father Samuel Palmer senior. Browning's mother, Sarah Anna, was laid to rest there in 1849.[1]

In 1839, the London Cemetery Company purchased the freehold of Nunhead Hill from Richard Edmonds (1789-1855) and others. Edmonds, a director of the ill-fated Deptford Pier Company, owned property at Nunhead and in neighbouring Hatcham.[2] The site comprised over 130 acres of arable, pasture, and meadowland, together with a cottage, barn, stable, cattle and cart sheds - all part of the former Shard estate.

Around 52 acres were set aside for a cemetery and a new road was laid out to connect the cemetery with Deptford Lane (now Queen's Road), Peckham in one direction and Nunhead Lane and Peckham Rye in the other. The remaining acreage, not being required for cemetery purposes, was sold to London merchant, Henry Ewbank of Denmark Hill, Camberwell, for the sum of £15,000.[3]

The new cemetery was enclosed and laid out with winding gravel paths and thickly planted with specimen trees and shrubs. Two substantial gate lodges were built on either side of the main entrance to provide a general office and accommodation for the cemetery superintendent and his family. The lodges were designed in the Neo-classical style with Grecian detail and chimney stacks resembling sepulchral monuments.

Two temporary chapels were erected. The Episcopal chapel was constructed over a vaulted catacomb chamber and the Dissenters' chapel was built on unconsecrated ground. Three unusual cylindrical shaft catacombs were constructed together with a range of 14 public burial vaults on the eastern side of the cemetery, and a single shaft catacomb was constructed near the temporary Dissenters' chapel. The landscaping and buildings, together with the Portland stone classical gate piers ornamented with cast-iron upturned torches, were the work of James Bunstone Bunning.

The Company's Southern Station, known as the Nunhead Cemetery of All Saints, was consecrated by the Right Revd Charles Richard Sumner, Bishop of Winchester, on Wednesday, 29th July 1840, in the presence of Henry Kemble, MP for East Surrey, and the directors of the London Cemetery Company, including the Revd Dr Russell and Michael Blount.

Eight acres in the western corner of the cemetery were left unconsecrated for the burial of Dissenters and others in accordance with the London Cemetery Company Act of 1836.

Nunhead's first few years in business

In 1840, when Nunhead Cemetery was nearing completion, George Collison, the Secretary of Abney Park Cemetery in north London, who naturally enough wanted to promote the merits of his own cemetery, wrote:

> I believe this Company (the London Cemetery Company) has obtained a site for their southern cemetery at Nunhead Hill, near Peckham, and that the ground is enclosed, and will shortly be consecrated. The success of this portion of their project must be very problematical, as the Nunhead Station is within two miles of the South Metropolitan Cemetery at Norwood, and which it will be impossible for the former to excel, and hardly to compete with, in beauty of prospect, style of architecture, or the convenience of the practical details and general arrangements.[4]

At first, Collison's observations proved to be correct, because only six burials took place in the first six months, and just 56 burials were recorded for the whole of 1841, several of which were in the cheaper class of common or communal graves. By 1842, however, business had started to pick up and 135 burials were recorded for that year.[5]

The burial rights to the first grave (square 141) were purchased in July 1840 by George Long Shand, a sail and tarpaulin maker of Bermondsey, for the burial of his two infant daughters, Ann Sophia and Georgiana. Shand was no doubt sickened by the dreadful state St Olave's, his local churchyard, which continued to be used for burials despite being indecently overcrowded. There had been reports of human remains being un-covered and left above ground. The beautifully landscaped Nunhead Cemetery, set in the Surrey countryside just a few miles south of Shand's home in Bermondsey, must have seemed like heaven on earth when com-pared to the hellish St Olave's churchyard.

The first interment in the unconsecrated ground was that of Margaret, wife of the Revd John Baptist Austin, a local Dissenting minister of Gold-smith House, Peckham, and Nun Green Chapel, Nunhead. She was buried in November 1840 in grave number five (square 161).[6]

Catacombs at Nunhead

The catacomb range beneath the temporary Episcopalian chapel, which became known as the Eastern Catacomb following the removal of the outer structure in 1844, contained compartments for 144 coffins in the main passage, several of which were occupied by 1841, along with 10 burial vaults and eight ante-rooms.[7] The two ante-rooms on either side of the main passage nearest the entrance to the catacomb range were pur-chased in 1852 and 1859 respectively by the Clarke family of Covent Garden, and three ante-rooms were used as public vaults. Another was purchased by the Governor of the Bank of England in 1933 to receive the human remains exhumed from the Bank garden (former churchyard of St Christopher-le-Stocks). The remaining ante-rooms were never used.

Of the four cylindrical shaft catacombs only two were brought into use. The shafts were excavated to a depth of around 16 feet and contained 30 burial cells in each. Shaft No 1 adjoined the Eastern Catacomb, and Shaft No 2 was situated in the Dissenters' Section at the confluence of two roads near the West Lodge. Both shafts contained a few coffins by 1843. They were not very popular, however, and most of the burial cells remained empty. Shafts Nos 3 and 4, and the series of 14 public vaults on the north eastern (consecrated) side of the cemetery were never brought into use and were demolished.[8]

Stone works set up outside Nunhead Cemetery

The first monumental mason to set up his stone works near Nunhead Cemetery was Henry Daniel (1805-67). According to the inscription on his substantial monument in the cemetery he was 'for many years con-nected with the cemeteries at Highgate and Nunhead'. Daniel built him-

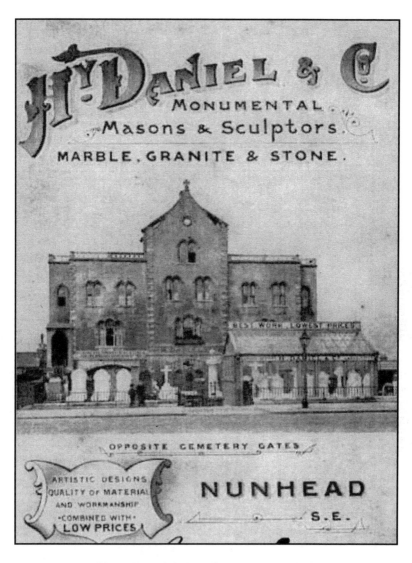

Henry Daniel & Co, advertisement c.1870

self a handsome house opposite the main entrance to Nunhead Cemetery called 'Church House'. Pevsner described it as 'the oddly gaunt and earnest Gothic edifice of Messrs Daniels'.[9] Two early gravestones at Nunhead bear the legend 'Daniels, masons to the cemetery.' After his death the firm prospered for another 100 years before eventually ceasing business in 1969.

Benjamin Joslin (d.1877), monumental mason and sculptor of Peckham Rye, claimed to be 'Mason to the London Cemetery Company' on his letterhead of 1868. Several members of the Joslin family were employed as gravediggers at Nunhead.

David Cripps Preston JP (1842-1925), stonemason and sculptor, owned a large stone works close to the cemetery. He was a proprietor of the London Cemetery Company and a regular attendant at General Meetings. A Nonconformist, he specialised in memorials to Dissenters, many of which may be seen in the unconsecrated ground at Nunhead, including his own monument, originally erected to the memory of his wife.

Directors of the London Cemetery Company give evidence before the Select Committee on the 'Effect of Interment of Bodies in Towns'

In April 1842, James Anderton (1752-1868), a solicitor and a member of the Common Council in the City of London, who served on the Board of the London Cemetery Company for many years before resigning due to failing health in 1867, was called to give evidence before the Select Committee on the Improvement of Health of Towns and the Effect of Interment of Bodies in Towns. When questioned by William Alexander Mackinnon MP, the Chairman of the Select Committee, Anderton said he had been to Paris and had seen a 'marked distinction' between the burying of the dead in that place and the burying of the dead here. While passing through St Margaret's churchyard in Westminster he had noticed several skulls and bones thrown out with putrid flesh. When asked about the general state of the churchyards in the metropolis, he said it was his opinion that they ought not to be permitted to exist any longer. He went on to say 'I always considered that the churchyards in this country being made into thoroughfares, boys playing at marbles and such things, was quite disgraceful'. He said he would prohibit the burial of all classes, rich or poor, in the existing churchyards and in churches too, if he could, which, of course, would have benefited the commercial cemeteries, such as those at Highgate and Nunhead of which he was a proprietor.

Anderton's colleague, the Revd Dr John Russell (1787-1863), Rector of Bishopsgate, and for many years Chairman of the London Cemetery Company, was also called to give evidence before the Select Committee and described the practice of burial in populous places as 'sickening and horrible'. The surgeon and burial reformer, George Alfred Walker, was also called to give evidence before the Select Committee, just as he had done two years previously.[10]

In 1843 the London Cemetery Company closed its office in Moorgate and opened a new Head Office at 15 New Bridge Street, Blackfriars. For a brief period the Company also had a branch office at 281 Regent Street in London's fashionable West End.[11]

Two permanent mortuary chapels built at Nunhead

In 1844 the temporary chapels at Nunhead were replaced by two permanent mortuary chapels, prior to which a competition had been advertised in *The Builder* and 65 designs submitted. According to the historian Edward Brayley (1773-1854) the designs of Thomas Little (1802-59) and William Hayward Brakspear (1818-98) were selected. Both chapels, however, have since been attributed to Little. The chapels were built in the decorated style of Gothic architecture which contrasted sharply with Bunning's neo-classical gate lodges and entrance piers.

The principal chapel (Anglican) is octagonal in form. Six sides of the octagon were fitted up with stalls for mourners. At the entrance was a 'carved oaken screen', and on the opposite side, a small reading-desk for the 'delivery of the burial service'. The ante-chapel was intended to be decorated in an 'arcade-like manner' for the reception of tablets and other memorials. The lofty entrance porch, which is open on three sides, enabled hearses and carriages to be drawn up within it. The embattled tower was surmounted at the corners by tall richly ornamented pinnacles, and the spacious vaults beneath the chapel were partially fitted up with catacomb compartments. The floor of the chapel contained an opening through which coffins could be lowered into the crypt. Access to the catacombs was by means of an entrance at the rear of the chapel. The cost was about £4,000. [12]

The Dissenters' chapel was destroyed during the Second World War. Smaller than the principal chapel, it was built on unconsecrated ground and lighted on each side by 'three hexangular-shaped windows', and at the end by a triple lancet window with a 'tracery head of quatrefoils and other ornaments'. The ante-chapel had a gallery above for the accommodation of 'spectators' and the chapel was neatly fitted up with stalls which were similar to those in the Anglican chapel. There was a small dressing room and vaults for catacombs beneath the building.

Another entrance was constructed at the western corner of the cemetery (next to the ancient Brockley footpath), which provided access to the unconsecrated ground and Dissenters' chapel.

Four years were to elapse before the first coffin was deposited in the vaults of the Anglican chapel,[13] and it took a further six years for the first coffin to be placed in the vaults of the Dissenters' chapel.[14]

In January 1847, Edward Buxton, who had been superintendent at Nunhead Cemetery since July 1840, succeeded Charles Burls of the Red House, Peckham Rye, as Secretary and Registrar to the Company.

Thomas Little's Anglican chapel
(note the castellated parapet on the carriage porch)

Cholera epidemic in south London

No less than 786 bodies were interred at Nunhead Cemetery in 1849, the highest annual number since 1840. The increase in burials was due to the cholera epidemic which was particularly severe south of the Thames. The outbreak was believed to have been caused by contaminated water supplied by the two principal water companies in south London - the Southwark and Vauxhall Water Company and the Lambeth Water Company - both of which obtained their water supplies direct from the Thames at Southwark and Lambeth respectively 'in a very imperfectly filtered condition'. In those days London's sewers discharged directly into the river and as a consequence the water was extremely foul. [15]

Compulsory purchase order served on Nunhead Cemetery

By 1851, in which year the radical statesman Joseph Hume MP (1777-1855) erected a splendid monument to the Scottish Political Martyrs in Nunhead Cemetery - another had been erected in Calton Hill Burial

Scottish Political Martyrs Memorial erected 1851
Dissenters' Ground, Nunhead Cemetery

Ground, Edinburgh, some years earlier - Nunhead Cemetery had become a fashionable burying ground patronised by wealthy City merchants and the gentry.

A dark cloud hovered over Nunhead, however, as it was one of two cemeteries earmarked for compulsory purchase under the Metropolitan Interments Act of 1850. This Act gave the General Board of Health the power to acquire all the commercial cemeteries in the London area.

In March 1851, the General Board of Health served compulsory purchase notices on both the Brompton and Nunhead cemeteries. The Board's estimate for Brompton was £43,836, but the West of London and Westminster Cemetery Company wanted £168,762. The Board valued Nunhead at £39,871, but the directors of London Cemetery Company, demanded £99,349. These amounts were later revised and increased to £75,000 and £42,000 respectively.[16]

The compulsory purchase order in respect of Nunhead was later withdrawn, much to the relief of the London Cemetery Company, when the Treasury instructed the General Board of Health to abandon the purchase of the two cemeteries. As a result, Brompton was the only London cemetery taken over by the Government at the insistence of the proprietors of the West of London and Westminster Cemetery Company. The Metropolitan Interments Act of 1850 was finally repealed in 1852.

The London Cemetery Company opens another cemetery at Highgate

In 1855 the London Cemetery Company opened its third and last cemetery - not in East London as originally planned - but a 19-acre extension to its Northern Station at Highgate on the east side of Swain's Lane.

The site once formed part of the estate belonging to Harry Chester JP (c.1806-69), educationist and President of the Highgate Literary and Scientific Institution. Another prominent Highgate resident, Jonah Smith Wells (c.1796-1876), stockbroker and future Chairman of the London Cemetery Company, was an acquaintance of Chester and a founder member of the Institution. Chester sold the site to the London Cemetery Company much to the annoyance of another Highgate resident, Miss Angela Georgina Coutts, later Baroness Burdett Coutts (1814-1906), who had wanted the land for a public park.[17] As a result, Miss Coutts's future relationship with the Board of the London Cemetery Company was far from amicable as we shall see.

The New Ground, or East Cemetery as it became known, was enclosed

31

and laid out with winding paths and connected to the Old Ground, or West Cemetery, by a tunnel constructed under Swain's Lane. Funeral services continued to take place in the chapels in the Old Ground, and the installation of a mechanical bier enabled coffins to be lowered into the tunnel by means of hydraulic pressure, and thence conveyed under Swain's Lane and into the New Ground.

The high cost of cemetery interment

Burial in the Company's cemeteries at Highgate and Nunhead was expensive. In 1856 the charge for a private grave excavated to a depth of seven feet was between three and five guineas (£3.15p to £5.25p) according to location. Graves in 'select' positions or excavated to a depth greater than seven feet cost considerably more. Extra ground could always be purchased by arrangement with the directors. The same charges for plots of a similar size were made by competing cemeteries at Kensal Green, Norwood, Brompton and Abney Park.[18]

A plot, nine feet by six feet, on which to construct a brick grave, could be purchased for 20 guineas (£21) at both Highgate and Nunhead, and the same amount was charged at the other commercial cemeteries in London.

A compartment in Terrace Catacombs at Highgate cost from ten guineas (£10.50p) to £17 for a single coffin, and from £55 to £94 for a space for six coffins. At Nunhead, a compartment for a single coffin in the Eastern Catacomb cost ten guineas (£10.50p), and a space in the chapel catacombs cost £20 guineas (£21) for a single coffin, and £110 for six coffins. A plot at the edge of Nunhead's central walk leading to the Anglican chapel cost £54.

The above rates were for the exclusive right of burial in perpetuity. Extra charges were payable for each interment, and for the opening and closing of graves and removal and replacement of monuments.

The fee for depositing a body in a catacomb compartment, brick grave or private vault, was five guineas (£5.25p), and interment in a private earth grave cost between two and three guineas (£2.10p to £3.15p). Only coffins of lead, stone, or asphalt were permitted in the Company's catacombs, vaults and brick graves.

Catacomb compartments were sometimes used for the temporary deposit of coffins pending the excavation of a private grave or the construction of a brick grave or vault.

Monuments add to the attractive appearance of cemeteries

Private brick graves and vaults were the most profitable and, according to the Board of Directors, most in keeping with the 'overall design' of their cemeteries. These 'superior' graves lined the roads which added to the attractive appearance of the cemeteries. The Company's regulations stipulated that monuments, not headstones, should be erected within 12 feet of the principal roads and other selected parts of the cemeteries, although this rule was relaxed towards the end of the 19th century to encourage more business.

Extra fees were payable for the use of a weather screen and for all burials taking place before two o'clock in the afternoon and after sunset. Covering a grave with turf cost another half-a-crown (12½p), and addi-

The Gargery family monument at Nunhead Cemetery c.1872

tional fees were payable for burials on Sundays. Sunday burials, however, were discontinued some time before 1855.[19]

No self-respecting Victorian gentleman would purchase a grave less than 14 feet deep, or capable of receiving at least eight dear departed members of his family, over which a substantial monument could be erected. If a family could afford it a brick grave or burial vault complete with step entrance, granite obelisk, and decorative metal railings situated on a prominent site, preferably at the edge of a road, was the most desirable.

The Company undertook, by sealed deed, to maintain the floral decoration of graves in perpetuity upon the payment of a fee determined by the Secretary. In accordance with the regulations in force at the time officers and manual employees were strictly forbidden to accept gratuities.

Burial of the poor

From the outset the London Cemetery Company provided for the burial of the poor, although at four guineas (£4.20p) the fee for burial in the public vaults at both Highgate and Nunhead was far from cheap. Interment in common or communal earth graves cost 30 shillings (£1.50p) per body and as much as two guineas (£2.10p) in selected locations. The burial of a child cost between 22 shillings (£1.10p) and 30 shillings (£1.50p).[20]

Memorials were not permitted on common graves; they were identified by a timber frame and numbered marker. It wasn't until the 20th century that individual memorials were allowed to be placed on common graves. Portable stone tablets not exceeding 12 inches square by four inches thick were permitted at Nunhead.

Originally large public monuments were erected at Highgate (West Cemetery) and at Nunhead, on which the names of persons buried in the Company's unmarked common graves could be recorded. The fee for a short inscription, i.e. just the name and date of death of the departed was one guinea (£1.05p). This was in addition the usual burial charges. The public monument at Highgate was demolished in April 1934 by order of the Board of Directors. Nunhead's public monument still exists, though the majority of names inscribed thereon are now barely legible.

Although the threat of compulsory purchase had disappeared along with Chadwick's General Board of Health, the new Burials Act of 1852 empowered the Metropolitan authorities (parish vestries) to elect local Burial Boards and to lay out cemeteries.

The Vestry of the Parish of Camberwell, in whose territory Nunhead lay, hastily appointed a Burial Board on receiving a letter from Lord Palmerston informing them that burials would no longer be permitted in the parish churchyard and vaults after 1st May 1854.

The Camberwell Burial Board met on the 27th April 1854, and Robert Alexander Gray DL, JP (1788-1871), the Chairman of the Burial Board, who made no secret of his dislike of the profit-making commercial cemeteries at Nunhead and Norwood, moved the following resolution:

That in the opinion of this Vestry it is the bounden duty of the living to make provision for the interment of the dead; that it had been found in parishes where the churchyard has been closed and no burial ground provided in lieu thereof, that the middle, artisan, and poorer classes have experienced considerable difficulty in burying their dead, the feelings of the poor disregarded, and the charges for interments beyond their limited means; that it is desirable and more economical that a parish so extensive and populous as Camberwell should have its own burial ground, and not be compelled to rely on the cemetery companies.[21]

Parish cemeteries threaten Nunhead's business

The Camberwell Burial Board instructed the Vestry Clerk, George William Marsden (1812-93), to find a suitable site for a cemetery and 31 acres of freehold land was found at Wood Lane (now Forest Hill Road), Peckham Rye, and purchased in August 1855 from the Trustees of Sir Walter St John's Charity. The site was duly laid out and enclosed, and the first burial took place on the 3rd July 1856.[22] In the following year the Burial Boards of the neighbouring parishes of St Paul's, Deptford, and Lewisham, opened cemeteries at Brockley. All three parish cemeteries were situated within a mile of Nunhead Cemetery.[23]

Between 1854 and 1858 over 17 parish cemeteries were established in the suburbs of London. Some local authorities, however, had no alternative but to enter into contracts with existing commercial cemetery companies. In 1854, the parish of St Saviour, Southwark, acquired a large burial plot in the London Necropolis which had recently opened at Brookwood, Surrey, rather than use the more expensive cemeteries at Nunhead and Norwood, and the Burial Boards of the parishes of Christ Church and St

George the Martyr, Southwark, acquired plots at Brookwood for the burial of paupers.[24] The wealthier residents of those parishes continued to be buried at Nunhead and Norwood.

In 1858 the Revd Dr James Hiles Hitchens DD, FRSL (1835-96) was appointed Nonconformist chaplain at Nunhead. He was pastor of the Peckham Rye Congregational Church in Linden Grove.

For several years the cheaper graves offered by the London Necropolis and parish cemeteries dramatically reduced the takings at Nunhead. In 1862, however, the directors were pleased to report that the takings at Nunhead were up by £200, and the number of burials by 40. Somewhat surprisingly Highgate's burials were down by 143.

Nunhead's new found prosperity was to be short-lived when the only main road between New Cross and the cemetery was left in an 'unacceptable state of repair' by the Metropolitan Board of Works, thus making the road impassable. The directors informed the shareholders that they had tried 'every means in their power to get the road adopted and maintained by the Parish of Camberwell without success'. (It was eventually taken over by the local authority in 1874). In 1863 further disruption was caused by the construction of a new railway line from Cow Lane, Peckham, to the Crystal Palace which obstructed the approach road to Nunhead Cemetery and prevented burials taking place.

The death of the Deputy Chairman and Chairman

William Samuel Jones, a director for many years, died in February 1862, aged 82. He was Master of the Crown Office, Queen's Bench, from 1843 to 1860, and had served on the Board of the London Cemetery Company since before 1846. A few months later Sir Benjamin Hawes, the Deputy Chairman, died suddenly aged 65. He too had been a director of the London Cemetery Company for many years. He was the eldest son of Benjamin Hawes (1770-1860), soap manufacturer, and a grandson of Dr William Hawes MD (1736-1808), founder of the Royal Humane Society. Sir Benjamin was MP (Whig) for Lambeth from 1832 to 1847, and Kinsale, Co Cork, from 1849 to 1852. Knighted in 1856, he was Under Secretary for War from 1857 to 1862. His wife, Sophia Macnamara, was the sister of Isambard Kingdom Brunel. According to Professor James Stevens Curl, Sir Benjamin was 'at the helm of the Board until Highgate Cemetery reached perfection'.[25]

The death of their 'esteemed' Chairman, the Revd Dr John Russell, in

June 1863 at the age of 76, came as another great shock to the Board. He had been a 'competent' Chairman and had 'filled the chair with much ability and advantage to the Company'. A former headmaster of the Charterhouse School and President of Sion College, he was also treasurer to the Society for the Propagation of the Gospel. He was Rector of St Botolph's, Bishopsgate, from 1832 to death, and a Canon of Canterbury Cathedral from 1827 to death. Dr Russell was succeeded by Jonah Smith Wells.

Suicide in Nunhead Cemetery

While walking in Nunhead Cemetery one fine Sunday evening in July 1864, Mrs Margaret Smith of the Old Kent Road, heard 'heavy breathing of a person in great pain'. On hurrying to the spot she saw a man lying by the side of a grave. She reported it to the superintendent who in turn called Dr George Webster. When the doctor arrived the man was dead. An inquest was held and it was found that the deceased had taken a large dose of potassium cyanide while of unsound mind. The dead man was James William Trist, aged 31, an unemployed insurance clerk of Walworth. It was said that since his mother's death, five years earlier, he had been acting rather strangely. He had been sacked for taking a holiday without leave, sold his furniture and turned his wife and young child out into the street. In the last letter to his wife he wrote: 'My dear wife, when you read these lines the individual who writes them will have taken the liberty of taking a view of the future state of society. I go to see my mother..... I believe now what Shakespeare says, that there is a method in madness. Farewell to this world. I am going to Nunhead'. He died with his head resting on the side of his mother's grave.[26]

By February 1865 the disruptive railway works had been completed and business was resumed as usual. Indeed, the takings at the Company's cemeteries were so exceptional that a Dividend of 12 shillings (60p) per share was announced, and the Company's officers were rewarded with a bonus of 5% on their salaries. The directors' remuneration was increased from £200 to £300 per annum.

3: THE BUXTON AFFAIR AND UPS AND DOWNS OF RECOVERY

In the summer of 1865 the Company suffered an 'unexpected and catastrophic' set-back when Edward Buxton, its 'respected and trusted' Secretary and Registrar, dropped dead on the 5th July at the early age of 49. He had attended a meeting of the Board earlier in the day and had complained of feeling unwell.

Edward Buxton, the son of Samuel Buxton of New Cross, was appointed Secretary and Registrar to the London Cemetery Company on the 19th January 1847. He was first employed as a clerk at the Head Office in 1836, and was appointed superintendent at Nunhead Cemetery in 1840. During his seven years as superintendent he had faithfully carried out his duties to the satisfaction of the Board, and had invented an ingenious system of excavating graves using hinged grave boards.[1]

Buxton was buried in his family grave (number 2883 square 68) at Nunhead Cemetery on the 11th July 1865, but his long association with the London Cemetery Company is not recorded on his tombstone for reasons which will soon become clear.

Shortly after the late Secretary's sudden demise, the Head Clerk, on preparing to visit the bank, discovered several ledgers in Buxton's office which aroused his suspicion. Careful examination of the books led to a disturbing discovery of falsified bank and pass books and a system of fraud and forgery that had been carried on by the late Secretary over many years. It later transpired that Buxton had kept two sets of books, and those placed on the table at Board Meetings were false. He had also been tampering with shares and issuing forged certificates.[2]

The Board seeks legal advice

The Chairman and directors, finding themselves in an unprecedented predicament, immediately sought urgent professional advice. John Bishop, a solicitor of 2 Tudor Street, Blackfriars, and Richard Lee, a public accountant and arbitrator of 5 Furnival's Inn, Holborn, were called in. Their task was to thoroughly scrutinise the late Secretary's books and papers, and advise on the current state of the Company's financial affairs.

At the General Meeting of Proprietors held at Radley's Hotel, New Bridge Street, Blackfriars, on the 10th August 1865, the whole sorry story of Buxton's devious activities were made known to the 47 proprietors present.

Buxton had left a will dated 1856 leaving his real and personal property for the benefit of his wife Elizabeth and son Henry, and appointed his wife and William Hine-Haycock as executors. William Hine-Haycock was a member of Hine, Robinson and Haycock, an old established legal firm in Charterhouse Square. He was also a proprietor of the London Cemetery Company. At first he objected to his name being associated with the affairs of Buxton 'who had so wholly lost his reputation', but later agreed to prove the will upon being indemnified against any liabilities that might arise.

On the promise that Buxton's estate should be distributed through the Court in Chancery, Hine-Haycock agreed to become defendant and account for all the assets which might occur.

Buxton had left a large estate and had promised his wife that she would be well provided for after his death. Sadly, as a result of his dishonesty, Mrs Buxton was left 'entirely destitute'. Her brother advised her to be extremely cautious about proving the will and recommended that she should wait at least six months before doing so. The directors, on the other hand, were anxious to settle the matter as quickly as possible for any delay in proving the will would have endangered a contract entered into by Buxton in the sale of a valuable property to which he was entitled.

The directors moved swiftly and succeeded in persuading Buxton's distraught widow to give up her claim on her husband's estate - despite her brother's advice - in return for an ex-gratia payment of £1 per week for 10 years. This agreement, not being within the powers of the Board, made the directors personally liable for the payment.

Thomas Britten Fenn (d.1880) of 29 Daniel's Road, Nunhead, was appointed Secretary 'pro tempore', and David George Davies Matthews took over as permanent Secretary on the 31st July 1865. His appointment was unexpectedly brief, however, for he died within a few weeks of taking up his post. He was succeeded by William Walton (1828-95), a Peckham man born and bred, whose difficult task it was to put the Company firmly back on its feet.

A new Register of Shareholders is prepared

At the General Meeting of Proprietors which took place at Radley's Hotel on the 7th February 1866, it was reported that the Board had issued circulars requesting all parties to bring in their share certificates. It was noted in the Minutes that the Board's request had been successful and all certificates received had been lodged at the Head Office. The 67 shareholders present, representing 6,731 shares, passed a resolution authorising the Board to compromise with those creditors who might prove against Buxton's estate and a revised 'Register of Shareholders' was prepared.

The directors and 36 shareholders representing 3,255 shares attended the General Meeting at Radley's Hotel on Wednesday 8th August 1866. A statement of accounts was prepared and sent to everyone whose name appeared in the revised 'Register' and it was hoped that a sufficient number would be brought together in order to carry on the business of the Company. The revised capital of the Company was fixed at £132,768 consisting of 16,596 shares at £8 each.

Sundry minor works were carried out at both Highgate and Nunhead in order to keep the Company's grounds in 'an efficient state of repair before the public'.

Major Charles Lestock Boileau resigned from the Board in 1866 due to poor health - he had been a director for over 20 years. A retired Major of Arms, Boileau resided at Castelnau House, Barnes, Surrey, which he had built and named after his family's former estate of Castelnau de la Garde in France. His ancestors were Huguenots who had fled to England to escape religious persecution and settled at Mortlake. Despite citing poor health as his reason for resigning from the Board he went on to live for another 23 years, dying in 1889 aged 88.

Another resignation that year was that of the Revd Dr Hitchens, Nunhead's Nonconformist chaplain. He was succeeded by the Revd Thomas Cole (1822-1902) of Nunhead Baptist Church, who went on to officiate at the cemetery for another 30 years.[3] Both gentlemen are buried in their family graves in the Dissenters' section at Nunhead.

The Suit for the Administration of Buxton's Estate is brought to a close

By 1867 the Suit for the Administration of Buxton's Estate had been brought to a close. The amount received out of the Court of Chancery was £2,617, and after deducting the accountant's and solicitor's fees, the net proceeds to the Company amounted to just £2,558. This was considerably less than the estimated £18,000 misappropriated by the late Secretary.

A vote of thanks was proposed by George Hammond Whalley MP (1813-78) for the 'efficient and courteous' manner in which Hine-

Haycock had performed the 'unpleasant yet most important duties of Executor' in the Administration in Chancery of Buxton.

William George Durnford, a solicitor and parliamentary agent of Parliament Street, Westminster, a large shareholder, was elected auditor at the General Meeting on 13th February 1867. His appointment was extremely brief, however, for he died at his residence, Feltham House, East Molesey, Surrey, on 28th April 1867, aged 58. He was buried in his family grave at Nunhead. At the same meeting the Company's 'esteemed and long serving director' James Anderton resigned from the Board because he found the duties 'too onerous' for his declining strength. He died at his residence in Dulwich in the following year aged 86, and was buried at Highgate.

In 1867, Philip Charles Hardwick (1822-1892), architect to the Bank of England, purchased three empty burial vaults on the south side of the Eastern Catacomb at Nunhead. The Bank of England had been built on the site of the demolished church of St Christopher-le-Stocks and the vaults were required to receive 23 cases of human remains removed from the former crypt of the church.[4]

Fewer deaths in the autumn and winter months of 1867 meant takings were down at all cemeteries. The Chairman thought the low death rate, which continued well into the following year, was probably due to, amongst other things, 'the sanitary improvements working out their beneficial results in the Metropolis'.

Also in 1867, a large increase in the parish rates at Nunhead, and the necessary expenditure required in improving the drainage and road surfaces at both Highgate and Nunhead, reduced the amount of profits available to be paid as dividends to shareholders.

Survival and recovery

Despite the considerable damage caused by Buxton's nefarious activities, the Company survived, albeit with some difficulty, and resisting the fierce competition from the parish cemeteries, continued to attract business from the wealthy classes.

Colonel John Harrison Allan (1820-82), of the Royal London Militia, who had buried his father at Nunhead in 1865, subsequently purchased a large piece of land on which to construct a new family vault. He paid £300 for the ground and commissioned Matthew Noble (1818-76), the sculptor, to carry out the work. The magnificent monument, loosely based on the Payava Tomb at Xanthos, was completed in 1867. Unfortunately the cost of construction is not known, but the massive granite tomb is possibly the most expensive ever erected at Nunhead.

Colonel Allan was probably responsible for the design. An enthusiastic amateur archaeologist, and a member of the Egyptian Society of Cairo and Athenian Archaeological Society, he had travelled extensively throughout Europe and the Middle East.[5]

Rather sadly, the monument was seriously damaged by vandals in the 1970s, and one of the two life-sized marble statues of semi-draped reclining female figures disappeared without trace. The other, toppled to the ground, has been defaced beyond recognition.[6]

John Allan's tomb in Nunhead Cemetery

In 1868 the Company's Bye-Laws were modified. It was decided that at least ten days before every General or Special Meeting the proprietors should be notified by letter of any changes in the direction, and no candidate should be eligible for election unless written notice had been received by the Secretary at least three weeks before the day of the election. It was also resolved that only one share certificate would be issued and held by each proprietor.

Also that year Michael Joseph Blount resigned from the Board. He told his colleagues that having reached the age of 84 he was feeling too old to continue. He died a few weeks later having been a director for 25 years. The Deputy Chairman, Thomas Bridge Simpson, remarked that he was 'an efficient and regular attendant at the Board'.

In 1869, the Buxton scandal raised its ugly head when William Hine-Haycock was obliged to defend a Bill filed against him by a Mr Gibbs, a former creditor, who in common with others had accepted 15 shillings (75p) in the pound in respect of the fraudulent shares. The Bill, much to the relief of Hine-Haycock and the Board, was dismissed with costs and the whole sorry Buxton saga was finally laid to rest.

The Secretary, William Walton, who had taken on the challenging task of running the Company after Buxton's death and at the most difficult period in its history, was rewarded with a substantial pay rise which increased his salary to £350 per annum.

The commercial cemeteries were assessed on a profit basis and the parish rates formed a large item in the Company's expenditure. In 1870 the new Valuation (Metropolis) Act threatened to increase the already excessive rates paid at Highgate. The directors appealed and succeeded in obtaining a 'considerable' reduction in the amount of rateable value proposed. No increase was attempted at Nunhead. The Company's property was valued at £150,598. This figure included the Highgate and Nunhead cemeteries, their several buildings, and all unsold catacomb compartments and burial vaults.

Profits were down in 1872 due to a slight reduction in the receipts at Nunhead. However, at the General Meeting held at Anderton's Hotel in 1873, it was reported that the Company's business was of the 'usual steady reliable character' with custom at Nunhead especially on the increase and, as a consequence, the usual Dividend of five shillings (25p) per share 'free of income tax' was announced.

The Board agree to purchase the Company's City office

At the Special General Meeting of Proprietors which took place at the Salisbury Hotel, Salisbury Square, Fleet Street, on the 12th February 1873, the Board agreed to purchase the freehold of their Head Office at 29 New Bridge Street. The Company had occupied the same building since 1843, originally as leaseholders, and since 1868 as tenants-at-will of the London, Chatham and Dover Railway Company. The directors were given notice to quit in September 1872 'with the full assurance that no treaty could be entertained except for the purchase of the freehold'. The location of the Company's Head Office for the last 30 years was considered sufficient reason for remaining there, and the concentration of railways leading to the cemeteries at Highgate and Nunhead made it particularly desirable to own the building. Indeed, a new railway station had opened near Nunhead Cemetery as recently as 1871. The LC & DR Company wanted £10,000 for the building and the directors offered £8,000. Eventually £9,000 was agreed as the purchase price. A further £2,600 was spent on rebuilding and enlarging the premises with a view to letting out the additional space.[7]

General William Nelson Hutchinson (1803-1895) resigned from the Board in 1873 having been a director since 1865. Captain James Combes Giffard was elected in his place.

At the General Meeting held in February 1874, the death was announced of O'Bryen Bellingham Woolsey JP at the age of 80. Woolsey had served the Company for many years both as auditor and director, and also served on the Board of the General Cemetery Company (Kensal Green Cemetery) and the Victoria and Legal and Commercial Life Assurance Company of which he was Deputy Chairman.

That same year, George Hammond Whalley MP (1813-1878), a barrister-at-law and senior director of the London Cemetery Company, found himself on the wrong side of the law. Whalley, an enthusiastic supporter of the Tichborne claimant, wrote to the newspapers and was fined £250 for contempt of court. He was imprisoned in Holloway Prison for refusing to pay the fine and later released when his sister paid it for him.

Despite an unexpected outlay for gravel and repairs to the roads at Nunhead Cemetery in 1874, the takings there were exceptional.

Brick graves and vaults are the most profitable

As family fortunes were made, simpler graves were sometimes exchanged for something grander. In 1874, Mrs Hilary Nissen, stationer of Mark Lane, London EC, ran up a large bill when she upgraded her private earth grave at Nunhead to a brick grave. The cost was £73-15s-6d (£73.77½p), less an allowance of three guineas (£3.15p) for the old grave which was sold back to the Company complete with the head and foot stones, which reduced the cost of the new grave to £70-12s-6d (£70.62½p) - still a considerable amount in the 1870s.

Overgrown and neglected - the Nolloth tomb in 1973

In 1876, Colonel Peter Nolloth RM, of North Terrace, Camberwell, exchanged his family's brick grave at Nunhead for a new burial vault complete with step entrance. The ground for the new vault alone cost £31 plus £21 for the extra ground required to build the step entrance. Brickwork for the vault cost £31 and the step entrance (constructed in cement) cost another £21. Removing five coffins, including those of his parents and brothers, from the old grave and placing them in the new brick vault, cost another five guineas (£5.25p). The total cost, including extra charges for excavations, a stone landing, iron coffin bearers, and entry of the burial grant in the ledgers, came to a total of £125 less a reduction of £20 for the old brick grave. The colonel's bill did not include the cost of a new memorial comprising a massive canted granite ledger complete with lengthy inscription, exterior steps, corner posts and gun metal chains. The empty brick grave was renumbered 15691 and sold to Mrs Mary Drew for the interment of her husband, the Revd George Smith Drew MA, FRGS (1818-1880), of Holy Trinity Church, Lambeth.

General Meetings now held in the Company's Head Office

On the 10th February 1875 the General Meeting of Proprietors took place in the newly refurbished Head Office, previous to which the proprietors had always met in hotels. Although present, the Chairman, Jonah Smith Wells, was unable to take the chair due to his increasing deafness, and his deputy, Thomas Bridge Simpson, was called to the chair. It was reported that after writing off the remainder of the outlay on the greenhouse at Nunhead, viz: £72, and a further £75 from the 'Furniture Account', the net profits fully provided for the payment of the usual Dividend of five shillings (25p) per share.

The resignation from the Board of the Revd Dr James William Vivian, due to his continued indisposition, was announced by the Chairman and much regretted by his colleagues. Dr Vivian had served the Company as auditor since the 1840s and as a director since 1865. He died the following year aged 91 years. His place was filled by John Kinnersley Hooper (1823-1885), wine merchant of Tooting Common, who resigned from the Board after three years.

One of the directors in attendance that day was George Hammond Whalley MP, whose last appearance was two years earlier. Unsurprisingly, there is no mention of Whalley's prolonged absence from meetings in the Company's Minutes, nor that of his brush with the law and subsequent, albeit brief imprisonment for contempt of court.

Another brief period of prosperity

By 1876 business was 'booming' in every direction. The largest receipts since 1862 were reported at the Company's cemeteries and the takings at Nunhead were exceptionally large. A Dividend of five shillings and sixpence (27½p) was announced, and the Secretary, superintendents, and staff at the Head Office were each rewarded with a handsome bonus of 10%.

Flowering, that is the decorating of graves with flowers and plants, had become increasingly fashionable by the 1870s, and now formed a lucrative side of the Company's business. In order to cope with the demand for fresh cut flowers, new greenhouses were erected on a vacant site behind the Anglican chapel at Nunhead

Lausanne Road (formerly a part of Cemetery Road) was completed by the parish from Queen's Road, Peckham, right up to the gates of Nunhead

46

Superintendent's Residence (East Gate Lodge) Nunhead Cemetery

Cemetery. The improved access attracted many new customers from the densely populated districts of New Cross, Rotherhithe and Deptford.

The East Gate Lodge (superintendent's residence) at Nunhead was enlarged at a cost of £370. The extension was in keeping with Bunning's designs and included an additional chimney in the same style. The only departure from the original neo-classical design was the erection of a typically Victorian bay window on the extension.

The exterior of the Eastern Catacomb at Nunhead was also repaired and its general appearance was much improved.

Jonah Smith Wells died on 27th May 1876, aged 80. He had been a director of the Company since before 1846, and Chairman since 1864. He was succeeded by Thomas Bridge Simpson, a London merchant, and a Lieutenant for the City of London. The vacancy thus created was filled by James Pateshall Jones, candle and soap maker of Fenchurch Street, who resigned from the Board after four years.

The death of Henry Hill, a director since 1866, was announced in

1876. He had served as Deputy Chairman and was described in the Company's Minutes as 'for 10 years past an active and zealous member of the Board'.

Decline in grave sales due to the economic depression

In 1878, following a brief period of prosperity, takings at Nunhead and Highgate were down. The Chairman blamed the depression in the country for the decline in the sale of graves. The charges for brickwork and the excavation of graves were increased due to a rise in the cost of labour and materials.

Also that year, the death of George Hammond Whalley was announced. Whalley, a barrister-at-law and MP for Peterborough, had been a director for over 32 years.

The severe winter of 1878/9 and the prolonged wet spring of 1879 required a sizeable outlay to repair the roads in all the Company's cemeteries and to keep the grounds in good order.

At the General Meeting held on 4th February 1879, Bryan Donkin (1835-1902), an eminent civil engineer, whose family had been connected with the Company since its early years, was elected auditor.

The Chairman, Thomas Bridge Simpson, who had been ill for several

Tomb of Thomas Bridge Simpson, Chairman, London Cemetery Company 1876-1879

months, died at his residence, Rutland Lodge, Brixton, on 18th May 1879, aged 89 years. He had been a director of the London Cemetery Company since before 1846; Deputy Chairman in 1867; and Chairman of the Board since 1876. Despite his short tenure as Chairman, Simpson was greatly valued by his fellow directors for 'his uniform urbanity and zeal for the interests of shareholders'. He was succeeded by Captain James Combes Giffard, a former officer in the Madras Native Infantry.

Simpson's son Frederic, who had been a member of the Board since 1874, died just one year later aged 65 years. Both gentlemen were laid to rest in the family vault at Nunhead.

In 1880 the Burial Laws Amendment Act was passed which allowed Nonconformist ministers to officiate at funerals in consecrated (Church of England) ground.[8] The directors of the London Cemetery Company informed their shareholders that the new Act did not apply to their cemeteries but, being anxious to protect the interests of the Company, agreed they would not object to Dissenters being buried in consecrated ground provided permission was first obtained from the Secretary. Funeral services, however, would continue to be held in the Dissenters' chapel.

William Samuel Jones MA, barrister-at-law, son of William Samuel Jones (1779-1862), a former director, was elected to the Board on the 10th February 1880 in place of the late Peter Bunnell (1801-1879) who had served the Company as auditor from 1867 to 1876, and as director from 1876 to death.

At the General Meeting held on 3rd August 1880, Bryan Donkin resigned as auditor. He was Chairman of Bryan Donkin & Co Ltd, and brother-in-law to Edwin Bedford, a former director of the London Cemetery Company. His father, John Donkin (1802-1854), and his grandfather Bryan Donkin FRS (1768-1855), an eminent civil engineer, are both buried at Nunhead.

It was reported that business at Nunhead was poor due to the continuing depression, increased competition from the parish cemeteries, and the reduced death rate. The Chairman said the Company's profits were also affected by a fall in the sale of brick graves in favour of the cheaper earth graves and the tendency of the middle classes to use the parish cemeteries.

Third class of private grave introduced at Nunhead

An experiment to encourage more sales at Nunhead was tried in 1881. A third class of private grave was introduced at a much reduced price, and the charge for common (communal) interment was reduced to meet the requirements of the large working class neighbourhood that had sprung up around the cemetery.

In the winter of 1881/2 the interior of Nunhead's Anglican chapel was redecorated at a cost of £100 and the original brick culvert drains were replaced by glazed stoneware pipes. Additionally, all the main roads in the cemetery required resurfacing.

Despite a substantial increase in the overall net profits as a result of lowering the prices at Nunhead, 1882 was a particularly miserable year for the Company. At the General Meeting held on the 7th February the Chairman, Captain Giffard, announced that the Company was involved in a law-suit under an action brought by Baroness Burdett-Coutts of Holly Lodge, concerning a section of the boundary wall at Highgate which was her ladyship's property. The wall had come crashing down during a particularly severe storm on the 28th February 1881.

Also that year the Vestry of Camberwell demanded £312 towards paving a new road (Limesford Road) adjacent to Nunhead Cemetery, and essential repairs were carried out to the interior of the Dissenters' chapel at Nunhead and both gate lodges repaired at a cost of £208.

Fortunately, gardening continued to be a lucrative side of the Company's business. Receipts for the sale of plants and flowers amounted to £1,394 at Highgate and £966 at Nunhead, as against £1,321 and £892 in the previous year.

Efficient and careful management aids recovery

By 1883 the takings at the Company's cemeteries had improved significantly. Somewhat surprisingly, Nunhead was the best paying of the cemeteries with profits in excess of £653 compared with just £187 at Highgate.

Captain Giffard took a personal interest in the upkeep of the Company's property and made it his business to inspect the cemeteries at least once a month - usually at a date unknown to the superintendents and their staff - to ensure everything was in perfect order. He claimed to have never once found a member of staff absent from his post or neglecting his duty during these surprise visits.

Despite an increase in the number of burials at Nunhead since the introduction of third class graves and reduced charges for common interments, the Board came to the conclusion that the end result was merely an increase in the workload and damage to roads and plant, without any appreciable increase in receipts. The experiment, therefore, was abandoned after just 12 months and the former tariff for interments was resumed.

Some experiments, however, benefited the Company. The acquisition of a horse and cart at Nunhead proved to be an invaluable asset, and horses and carts were purchased at Highgate. It was claimed that the Company's carts were used more often than those under the old hired system and as a result the cemetery grounds were kept in much better order.

With regard to the collapsed boundary wall belonging to Baroness Burdett-Coutts, the court ordered the London Cemetery Company to rebuild the wall, but refused to grant the injunction applied for by the plaintiffs which, according to the Chairman, was the main reason the Board chose to defend the action in the first place. The costs of both sides, £796 plus £150 to rebuild the wall given as 'damages', fell on the Company, even so, the directors felt the outcome was satisfactory. The Chairman explained that, heavy as the costs were, the loss would have been far greater had the action been undefended, for it would have forced the Company to remove several existing graves and make other 'serious and expensive' alterations.

At the General Meeting of Proprietors held on 5th February 1884, Stephen de Gurbs was called to the chair in the place of Captain Giffard who was indisposed. The Secretary then presented the Report of the Directors which was very gloomy indeed. The General Revenue Account showed the smallest amount of net profit made for many years, which the directors believed was partly due to 'the continued depression in the trade generally and the consequent indisposition to spend more money than necessary'. The main reason, the directors concluded, was the 'very low rate of mortality during the last six months of 1883' which had resulted in 'the smallest total of gross receipts' at the Company's cemeteries during the last 16 years.

Captain Giffard died on the 27th February 1884, aged 63 years, having chaired his last meeting on 31st July 1883. James Combes Giffard was a son of Admiral John Giffard RN (1766-1855), and younger brother of Sir George Markham Giffard PC, QC (1813-70), Lord Justice of Appeal. A former officer in the Madras Native Infantry, Captain Giffard had served on the Board of the London Cemetery Company since 1873 and as Chairman since 1879. As Chairman he always took a personal interest in the care and upkeep of the Company's cemeteries, and was laid to rest on the summit of the hill in Nunhead Cemetery (grave 17566 square 85).

At the General Meeting of Proprietors held on 5th August 1884, Captain Giffard's successor, William Samuel Jones, a barrister-at-law and magistrate, referred to his predecessor in 'highly eulogistic terms'. At the same meeting the new Chairman was anxious to dispel rumours that Highgate Cemetery was full and urged members to deny any such comments.

Herbert Hardwick Trist, a wine merchant, was duly elected to fill the vacancy on the Board created by the death of Captain Giffard.

The deaths of John Curtis and Edwin Bedford within a week of each other came as a great shock to the Board. Both gentlemen had been 'eminently useful on the direction' and were much esteemed by their colleagues. John Curtis, a so-

Grave of Captain James Combes Giffard, Chairman, London Cemetery Company 1879-1884

licitor, was brother-in-law to Sir Benjamin Hawes, a former Deputy Chairman of the Company. A large shareholder, he was elected a director in 1868 and was one of the Company's oldest Board members at the time of his death which took place at Rothesay, Isle of Bute, on 23rd August 1884 aged 82. His nephew, Edwin Bedford, also a solicitor, was the son of Francis Octavius Bedford (1784-1858), the distinguished architect, and brother-in-law to Bryan Donkin MICE (1835-1902), a former auditor of the London Cemetery Company. A member of the Board since 1878, he died at Westbourne Terrace, London, on 30th August 1884, aged 57.

A net profit of £4,468 was announced for the first six months of 1885 which was £400 in excess of the average profits for the past ten years. The Chairman remarked that the increase was unusual considering the sale of burial rights had been less than average. He went on to say that the increase in profits had resulted from efficient and careful management.

The profits for the last six months of 1885 dropped dramatically, however, mainly as a result of the low death rate prevailing in London at that time.

Discounts to undertakers is stopped

At the General Meeting of Proprietors held on 2nd February 1886, John Glazier, a shareholder and undertaker, drew the attention of his colleagues to the fact that the directors had stopped giving discounts to undertakers. He claimed that business at both Nunhead and Highgate was suffering as a result. The Chairman was quick to point out that the withdrawal of discounts was a considerable saving to the Company, and went on to say that he was not convinced that the 'undertaking trade' had done the Company any harm as a result of stopping the discounts.

George Robert Bengough, a director, who also served on the Board of the General Cemetery Company, assured shareholders that a large decrease in business had been felt at Kensal Green too, even though that cemetery continued to give discounts to undertakers.

The Chairman announced that the Board had signed a contract with the United Telephone Company Limited and the Head Office at New Bridge Street was now in direct communication with the cemetery offices at Nunhead and Highgate.

Also in 1886, the Vestry of Camberwell had demanded £379 for paving part of public footway along Nunhead Cemetery's boundary wall in Linden Grove. After considering the matter the directors came to the conclusion that the footpath was not their responsibility and refused to pay.

The death of Mr Nicholson, a former employee, at the advanced age of 103, was received by the Board with a certain amount of relief, for he had been receiving the annuity of £100 for the past thirty years!

Some bays between the piers at Nunhead Cemetery are bricked up

In 1887 some of the cast-iron railings between the brick piers on Linden Grove were removed and the bays bricked up. The Chairman, William Samuel Jones, informed the Board that owing to adverse publicity a large piece of valuable unconsecrated land at Nunhead was un-saleable because mourners attending funerals at the Dissenters' chapel were frequently disturbed by unruly children and others causing a nuisance outside the railings. The west entrance, adjoining Brockley Footpath, was bricked up at

West entrance to Nunhead Cemetery, closed and bricked up in 1887

the same time because children were seen running in and out of the cemetery and upsetting grave owners and visitors. The Chairman assured shareholders that the cost of around £330 to complete the work would not affect profits.

Nunhead is worst paying cemetery

Despite discounts to undertakers being resumed in November 1886 and an acceptable increase in takings as a result, the parish cemeteries continued to have a detrimental effect on business, especially at Nunhead, and by 1888 it was the Company's worst paying cemetery.

The death of George Robert Bengough at the age of 82 was announced in 1888. He had served as auditor to the London Cemetery Company from 1877 to 1879, and was a director from 1879 to death. He also served on the Board of the General Cemetery Company (Kensal Green Cemetery), and was its Chairman between 1879 and 1882.

The employment of an extra stonemason at Nunhead, to put upright a great many headstones that were 'out of the perpendicular' much improved the appearance of the cemetery, and the Chairman informed shareholders that he was confident that these 'improvements' would attract more custom to Nunhead.

Edward Martin, 'a much respected employee' of the London Cemetery Company, died on 8th February 1889, aged 54 years. He had been superintendent at Nunhead Cemetery since 1865, during which time he had been a loyal and efficient member of staff. He personally carried out building and other work in the cemetery grounds thereby saving the Company 'a considerable amount of expenditure'. A dedicated and conscientious employee, Martin was 'always at his post and rarely took a holiday'. He had been unwell for several weeks prior to his death during which time the Secretary, William Walton, had carried out his duties. As a mark of their appreciation the directors granted Martin's widow an allowance of £1 per week for three years 'on condition that she did not take the allowance for granted and did not remarry'.

John Witty, Highgate's head gardener, was promoted superintendent in place of Martin, and Nunhead's head gardener (whose name is not recorded in the Minutes) was dismissed saving the Company 30 shillings (£1.50p) per week in wages. The Chairman said Witty was more than qualified for the post at Nunhead, for he had been head gardener at Highgate for 11 years during which time he had deputised when Highgate's superintendent, Frederick William Ta'Bois, was on leave or otherwise indisposed.

Nunhead's tariff is reduced to attract new business

In 1889 the receipts at Highgate were up and the receipts at Nunhead were down. In fact Nunhead's takings were the lowest in 22 years. The directors came to the conclusion that the increased competition by the neighbouring parish cemeteries had to be met with a reduction of the tariff, particularly for common interments. Common burials accounted for a large proportion of business at Nunhead, and to encourage custom from the poorer classes the charges for common interment were reduced to 30 shillings (£1.50p) for an adult, and 12 shillings and six pence (62½p) for a child.

By 1890 common graves at Nunhead were being excavated to a depth of 24 feet to contain as many as 40 coffins in each. Common graves dug to this depth were worth around £50 in fees to the Company, whereas a similar plot sold privately raised a mere £6 or so. One of the unused shaft catacombs was demolished and replaced by seven 20 feet deep common graves and a total of 170 bodies were buried in them.[9]

The modification and reduction of the tariff apparently paid off because when the Proprietors met on the 5th August 1890, the net profits announced for the last six months were £414 at Nunhead and £215 at Highgate.

At the same meeting the Chairman informed the shareholders that the Secretary, William Walton, had completed 25 years service, and went on to say that he had taken on the responsibility of 'practically reconstructing' the Company at the most difficult time in its history. He was, of course, alluding to the massive fraud perpetrated by Walton's predecessor, Edward Buxton. As a mark of their appreciation the directors awarded Walton a handsome present of 100 guineas (£105).

The interiors of both chapels at Nunhead and the exteriors of the two gate lodges required redecorating at a cost of £150. The Chairman emphasised that the work would not be charged against profits, but would be spread over the next five years as 'special outlay' in accordance with the usual procedure in such matters.

The 'better class' of grave more saleable at Highgate

At the General Meeting held on 3rd February 1891, an unnamed shareholder objected to the large amounts paid as 'commission' to undertakers and demanded the practice be stopped. The Chairman informed the disgruntled member that it would not be in the Company's interest to stop giving discounts to undertakers. It had been tried once before, he explained, and the business had suffered as a result.

Another suggestion that Highgate's tariff should be reduced was rejected without consideration. The Chairman explained that burial space at Highgate was becoming increasingly scarce, and those who purchased graves there were usually wealthy, therefore the 'better class' of grave was more saleable at that cemetery.

There was a problem at Highgate, however, which prevented the sale of valuable grave space. The Chairman informed the meeting that the tenants in the houses adjoining the lower ground were being offensive to grave owners and unruly children were causing distress to mourners and visitors by running amok among the graves. Indeed, the Chairman had personally witnessed several children darting in and out of the cemetery on more than one occasion. The directors gave the matter careful consideration and decided to remove the railings between some of the bays and brick them up. Similar action had been taken at Nunhead in 1887 which had solved the problem at that cemetery. The estimated cost was £300.

Economical management and influenza boosts profits

The Company was doing exceptionally well in 1891. The gross receipts were £12,547 at Highgate and £8,882 at Nunhead. It was noted that the improvement in the takings at Nunhead was mainly due to the reduction in charges at that cemetery. The Board had invested £2,000 in Home Railway 3% Debenture Stock, bringing the Company's total investments up to £23,247 which generated an income of around 5%.

Mausoleum in Highgate Cemetery

In 1892 the takings were up yet again. Receipts for the first six months at Nunhead were £9,256 - the highest ever recorded at that cemetery. In fact the Company's business had never been better, mainly due to the 1891/2 influenza epidemic.

The directors informed the shareholders that they gave their constant attention to the 'economical management' of their cemeteries and, although the expenses were necessarily higher than they were 20 years ago, 'there wasn't a single cemetery in London that was kept in a better condition, or was more efficiently run, than those at Highgate and Nunhead.' This they attributed to the continuing, and as to Nunhead, the increasing patronage secured. The Company's investments now stood at £27,200.

At the General Meeting held on the 2nd August 1892, the directors congratulated the shareholders and reported a balance of profit 'wholly unprecedented in the annals of the Company since its reconstruction in 1865'.

Despite the good news, a discontented shareholder wanted to know why the cemeteries were now closed on Bank Holidays, and on hearing the Chairman's explanation (not recorded in the Minutes) he complained that the notice given was much too short. The same shareholder had earlier made some critical remarks about Nunhead's gardening department.

Alexander Travers Hawes, a shareholder, proposed that a honorarium of 200 guineas each should be granted to the directors. His proposal was seconded and carried unopposed.

Stephen de Gurbs, a director since 1868, died on the 14th December 1892 at the advanced age of 92. He first served as auditor during a difficult period in the Company's history back in 1865, and was Deputy

Chairman for a time. In 1898 a memorial window was erected in the chapel of the University of Aberdeen by his widow, with an inscription describing him as 'Stephen, Baron de Gurbs'.

At the General Meeting held on 7th February 1893, three shareholders presented themselves for election to fill the vacancy created by the death of de Gurbs, viz: Maurice Chapman Anderson, Leonard Bonus and Alexander Travers Hawes. Messrs Anderson and Bonus later withdrew in favour of Hawes in view of his 'long standing' connection with the Company and the length of time since he first presented himself for a seat on the Board in 1888.

The directors reassured members that the Capital Account was not being diminished by the sale of the land as in some of the other proprietary cemeteries. They went on to explain that the accounts show that as the item 'Land, etc' on the assets side of the balance sheet is diminished, the item 'Investments' is increased, so that the shares, are not, as some might consider 'in the character of interminable annuity'.

In 1893 one of the unsold vaults in Highgate's Lebanon Circle was converted into a columbarium for the reception of cremated remains. The Company had not yet considered operating a crematorium of its own, nevertheless, the Board thought it advisable to accommodate those clients whose friends and loved ones were being cremated elsewhere. The ashes of two bodies cremated at Woking in 1886 were subsequently buried in family graves at Nunhead and Highgate respectively.[10] The first crematorium opened in Surrey at Woking in 1885, and this was followed by another at Manchester in 1892. London's Golders Green Crematorium was opened in 1902.

Towards the end of 1893 the Secretary's health 'entirely broke down', and the directors suggested he should try a voyage for the restoration of his health.

In 1894 the Company's old 'arch-enemy', the Vestry of the Parish of Camberwell, demanded £743 towards paving a new road (Limesford Road) on the south side of Nunhead Cemetery. The directors refused to pay and successfully defended the Company before a magistrate, but the Vestry appealed to a higher court which decided against the Company.[11] A shareholder suggested that it might have been advisable to approach the Vestry with a view to a compromise. The Chairman replied that it was most unlikely to find a soft spot in a Vestry's heart.

At the General Meeting held on 5th February 1895 Samuel Lovelock was called to the chair as William Samuel Jones was indisposed. The death of William Walton was announced and much regretted by the Board. Walton had been Secretary since August 1865. Thomas Stonnill, a clerk at Head Office, who had served as Acting Secretary during Walton's last illness, was appointed Secretary at the recommendation of the Chairman. His appointment was seconded and supported by two shareholders.

Another influenza epidemic at the beginning of 1895 boosted the Company's profits, and the Sale of Land (Investment) Account now stood at £30,337. In view of the Company's continuing success, the directors awarded themselves a rise of £100, increasing their total annual remuneration to £400.

The flowering side of the business continued to be popular with the public and, as a consequence, in 1896 additional greenhouses were built at Nunhead. A small section of the boundary wall at Nunhead had to be rebuilt by order of the London County Council.

Marcus Staunton Lynch Staunton, a director since 1881, died at Fulham on the 19th October 1896, aged 70. A barrister-at-law, he was the eldest son of George Staunton Lynch Staunton JP, DL, of Clydagh, Co Galway, Ireland. His place on the Board was filled by Maurice Chapman Anderson, solicitor and parliamentary agent.

A suggestion to construct a crematorium is turned down

At the General Meeting which took place at the Head Office on 2nd August 1898, Edward Day Boddington, a shareholder and undertaker's assistant, suggested it might be in the Company's interest to erect a crematorium in one of its cemeteries, provided it could be achieved without appealing to Parliament. The Chairman, William Samuel Jones, was far from enthusiastic. He argued that any such proposal would be met with much opposition from the shareholders and general public alike. Besides, the burial business was doing exceptionally well. Indeed, the Company's profits were the highest for 10 years - despite the low death rate.

By January 1899 the Sale of Land (Investment) Account had reached £37,310, and the Board reported that the cemeteries were in 'excellent order and condition' reflecting much credit on the staff.

The Secretary, Thomas Stonnill, died on 13th January 1899, aged 61. He was succeeded by Henry Martyn Dodd who had been a servant of the Company for 28 years.

At the General Meeting held on 1st August 1899, the Board reported a satisfactory result in the takings over the last six months, the net profit being £4,948. The Chairman attributed the rise to the flowering side of the business and the higher charges introduced for excavating graves. The salary of the directors was increased from £400 to £500 per annum.

Nunhead's chapels required maintenance which cost £180, and the construction of a deep drain, also at Nunhead, cost a further £248. The Board informed the shareholders that the additional ground thus made available could be used for common graves.

The Romanesque Stearns mausoleum in Nunhead Cemetery c.1970

The only surviving mausoleum in Nunhead Cemetery. It was constructed for the Stearns family of Twickenham by Doulton of Lambeth in 1901/2. There were just two deposits: Mrs Laura Stearns in 1902 followed by her son-in-law in the 1920s. The two bodies were removed in the 1930s and interred in a nearby earth grave. The mausoleum has remained unoccupied ever since. It was restored in 2000 and is now listed Grade II.

4: A NEW CENTURY, RENEWED PROSPERITY & TWO WORLD WARS

The first few years of the 20th century were among the Company's most prosperous. The net profit for the first six months of 1900 was £5,889 which was the largest figure for a decade.

The Chairman, William Samuel Jones, resigned in 1899, and died the following year at the age of 69. He was succeeded by Samuel Lovelock FCA, chartered accountant and a partner in the firm of Lovelock, Whiffin and Dickinson of 19 Coleman Street, London, EC.

Also in 1900, Samuel Lovelock's other partner, Henry William Sharp Whiffin FCA, a former Accountant General to the British Army, who had loyally served the London Cemetery Company as auditor since 1880, resigned owing to failing health. He died in 1904.

In 1901, Arthur Lowes Dickinson MA, FCA, another of Lovelock's partners, who had served as auditor to the London Cemetery Company since 1886, did not stand for re-election. He removed to the USA and became a senior partner in the firm of Price, Waterhouse and Company. He returned to England in 1913 and was knighted in 1919. He died in 1935 aged 75 years.

Nunhead's superintendent, John Witty, returned to Highgate following the resignation of Frederick William Ta'Bois, Highgate's superintendent since 1868. The superintendent's post at Nunhead was filled by Robert Forster, Highgate's head gardener, who was head gardener at Peterley Manor House, Great Missenden, Buckinghamshire, before joining the London Cemetery Company in 1896. Forster died at Radlett, Hertfordshire, on the 25th January 1924, aged 69, and was buried in his family grave at Nunhead. The Company's records do not specify when he ceased to be Nunhead's superintendent. His successor, Henry Charles Clements, predeceased him.

Improvements carried out at Nunhead in 1902 include heating the two mortuary chapels by means of a hot water apparatus installed in the crypts, and by planting over 100 trees on old unmarked graves.[1]

The only anticipated outlay at Nunhead in 1903 was for the purchase of another horse. A long serving director, Dr John William Hue FRCP, died on Christmas Eve 1903, aged 84. He had served on the Board for 38 years. His brother, Corbet Hue, barrister-at-law, died the following year aged 86. He had been a director for 25 years.

Old graves repossessed, repurchased, renumbered and resold

The recycling of old graves was practised by the London Cemetery Company throughout its existence. From time to time graves were repossessed under the Company's strict 'Rules, Regulations and Bye-Laws'. For example, in 1903 the burial rights to two early graves at Nunhead, numbers 4812 and 4828 respectively, both dating from 1857, were repossessed under Regulation 12 which stated that 'every monument, gravestone or other erection, shall be maintained in good order and condition by the owner, thereof, otherwise the right of burial shall be forfeited'. Although both graves contained human remains they were repossessed, renumbered and sold as new.

Old graves were sometimes repurchased by the Company. In 1855 Louisa Duggan of Rotherhithe was granted the burial rights to grave number 3642 in square 111 at Nunhead for three guineas (£3.15p). Five bodies were interred in the grave including the owner herself in 1890. The burial rights were subsequently transferred to a relative who sold the grave back to the Company for 30 shillings (£1.50p) in 1904, and received an additional allowance of 15 shillings (75p) for the old headstone. The grave was renumbered 27337 and sold as new despite still containing human remains.

Samuel Green, Nunhead's Postmaster, becomes Chairman

At the General Meeting held in August 1903, the Deputy Chairman, Samuel Green, was called to the chair due to the unexpected retirement of Samuel Lovelock through illness. In addressing the shareholders, Green said the Company was 'deeply indebted' to the retiring Chairman for his 'long and valuable services'. He felt sure that in so saying he expressed the unanimous voice of all his colleagues on the Board.

It was reported that the amount of business completed at Nunhead and Highgate during the past 12 months had compared favourably with the other London cemeteries, despite the unusually low death rate during the winter months.

The Board made an offer for the freehold of the Townshend Yard Nursery in Highgate High Street, and in 1905 the Company acquired the property for the sum of £1,500 along with another piece of land, and the entire site purchased from the Governors of Christ's Hospital was laid out as a nursery ground. The Chairman, Samuel Green, said the acquisition of

Townshend Yard was essential in operating the Company's large and steadily increasing flowering business.

Samuel Lovelock, who had stood down as Chairman in 1903, finally resigned from the Board in 1905. He was held in high esteem by the directors having served as auditor for 12 years before becoming a director. He had 'reformulated' the accounts when first taking office as auditor following the Buxton scandal in 1868, and had started the 'Sale of Land Investment Account'. As Chairman he had always promoted the interests of the Company and had gained the admiration and respect of his colleagues. He died at East Preston, Sussex, in 1913, aged 83.

In August 1907, Samuel Green reported a substantial increase in the takings at Nunhead amounting to £751 in excess of the corresponding period in 1906, which was £495 above the average of the last six years. Investments in the 'Sale of Land Account' now stood at £51,127, but for some undisclosed reason all particulars relating to future investments were dropped from the Shareholders' Minutes Book after 1908, by which time the amount had risen to £53,000.

Samuel Green died in November 1907 at the age of 65, and was laid to rest in Nunhead Cemetery (grave 18350 square 90). Green was for many years the sub-postmaster at 2 York Place, Nunhead Green, where he was also a chemist and stationer. He served as auditor to London Cemetery Company in 1884, and was elected a director in February 1885 and Chairman in 1903. He was succeeded by Alexander Travers Hawes JP.

Improvements carried out at Nunhead

In 1908 the stables at Nunhead were rebuilt, and a new path was laid around the Dissenters' chapel and new drains installed. Several paths in the cemetery grounds were narrowed to make more space available for additional rows of private graves.

One of the most impressive sights ever seen at Nunhead was the funeral of Sir George Thomas Livesey (1834-1908), industrialist and philanthropist, which took place on the 10th October 1908. Something like 7,000 people lined the route of the funeral procession all the way from the Old Kent Road to the gates of the cemetery. His monument, a simple red granite obelisk over a brick grave, occupies a prominent position on the east side of the main walk leading to the Anglican chapel.

In 1909 a major improvement at Nunhead was the construction of a much-needed entrance in Limesford Road. The new entrance provided

The funeral cortege of Sir George Livesey en route to Nunhead Cemetery 1908

access to the residents of the Newlands Estate at Peckham Rye and the new Waverley Park Estate which had been built on several fields east and south of Nunhead Cemetery.[2] A new road, which led to the gates, was constructed inside the cemetery and lined with Lombardy poplars. Sadly, by the late 1970s they were well past their prime and some came crashing down during a severe storm. The remaining trees were felled.

There were fewer graves excavated on the southern slopes of the cemetery and a substantial amount of ground remained unused well into the 1920s. A large piece of land in the southern corner of the cemetery was used as a nursery ground before being made available for burials, largely for common graves, in the 1940s and 1950s.

The share capital is reduced

1910 was a difficult year for the Company - the reduced rate of mortality in Greater London, and the inevitable reduction in the takings at the cemeteries was not good news for shareholders.

At the General Meeting held on the 28th July 1910, Edward Day Boddington, an undertaker, who had once proposed unsuccessfully that the

Company should consider building a crematorium in one of its cemeteries, commented on the Capital Account and proposed that the invested funds should be sold and the proceeds applied in reducing the share capital. His proposal was put to the meeting and, on this occasion, was carried unanimously.

At the Special General Meeting of Proprietors held at the Head Office on the 7th February 1911, Alexander Travers Hawes was called to the chair. The Secretary, Henry Martyn Dodd, read the advertisement appearing in *The Times* and *Daily Telegraph* convening the meeting, and after a few opening remarks by the Chairman explaining a new Bill before Parliament, the proposed Bill was read out and explained by the Company's solicitor. It was resolved that the new Bill 'to rearrange, reduce and fix the capital of the Company, and to confirm past issues of paid up shares and past distributions of capital and dividends, and to extend the Company's power to acquire and hold land, and for other purposes' be approved subject to such alterations as Parliament may think fit. The resolution was seconded by Mr Heard, a shareholder, and carried unanimously.

The Bill received the Royal Assent on 2nd June 1911. The capital of the Company was reduced from £132,768, consisting of 16,596 shares of £8 each, to £99,576, consisting of 16,596 shares of £6 each, and £2 per share was returned to shareholders.

Main entrance to Nunhead Cemetery as seen from Daniel's Road c.1911

Tragic Scouts buried at Nunhead

On the 10th August 1912 a funeral took place at Nunhead which attracted nationwide publicity, and was just as impressive as that of Sir George Thomas Livesey which had taken place four years earlier. This was the funeral of eight Boy Scouts who had lost their lives in a freak boating accident off Leysdown on the 4th August 1912. Winston Churchill MP, First Lord of the Admiralty, arranged for the boys' bodies to be brought up the Thames on board HMS *Fervent,* a Royal Navy destroyer, and according to press reports at the time, the Scouts were 'laid in state' in the parish church of St John's Walworth. Around 100,000 people passed through the church to pay their respects, and crowds of people lined the route of the funeral procession all the way from Walworth to Nunhead Cemetery. The body of a lad from the training ship *Arethusa,* who had lost his life in the same incident, was also recovered and buried with the Scouts. A memorial fund was set up by the *Daily Express* and a magnificent monument, designed by the architect Sir Giles Gilbert Scott (1880-1960), together with a life-size bronze figure of a mourning scout sculpted by Miss Lillie Read, was placed over the grave.[3]

Also that year, Henry Charles Clements, the superintendent at Nunhead, organised a major clean-up of his cemetery. Over the next three years more than a thousand old graves, many of which had been neglected or abandoned by their owners were made safe. Decayed and dangerous monuments were taken down, rickety old headstones demolished, and broken and rusty railings removed.[4]

Crematorium proposed for Nunhead

The subject of cremation, first raised by Edward Day Boddington in 1898, had occupied the attention of the Board for several years. In 1912 the directors decided the cost of building a crematorium would be 'much too much' for the Company to bear. Just one year later, however, a 'well-known architect' (not named in the Minutes) was consulted, and possible sites for the construction of a crematorium at Nunhead were considered. The Board was authorised to proceed with the project at a cost of no more than £4,000. Regrettably, with the outbreak of the First World War in 1914, the scheme was abandoned and, as a result, the London Cemetery Company lost out to the South Metropolitan Cemetery Company who opened south London's first crematorium at Norwood Cemetery in 1915.

Business as usual during hostilities

In 1915, despite the war raging in Europe, the Company was doing exceptionally well financially, even so, a proposal that the directors be awarded a bonus of £210 in appreciation of their work was objected to by an unnamed shareholder who argued that the motion should not have been proposed without prior notification. The Chairman agreed and the motion was withdrawn.

Writing in 1979, Mr F. E. Thompson of Daniel's Road, Nunhead, who started work at Nunhead Cemetery in 1915, recalled that the cemetery was a 'showpiece' in his day, attended by two uniformed gatekeepers wearing top hats. An enormous vase at the top of the broad walk (main avenue) was positioned so as to stop traffic going right up to the chapel. Originally, the two side roads (east and west crescents) were used by hearses and carriages. Behind the Anglican chapel there were seven greenhouses, and during the summer months, when they had been cleared of bedding plants, tomatoes and cucumbers were grown and sold to visitors.

When Mr Thompson started work in the cemetery there were two horses and carts. He recalled that close by the Limesford Road entrance were haystacks made by cemetery staff on a space cleared by scything. Every so often, a four wheeled wagon would be loaded with hay at four o'clock in the morning and carmen would make the journey to Highgate Cemetery. Each afternoon at four o'clock the staff would go round the roads in the cemetery and clear up horse droppings. The manure collected was used in the frames as hot-beds.[5]

Nunhead's superintendent, Henry Charles Clements, died in 1915 at the early age of 51. A local man, he was born in 1864 at Daniel's Cottages, Nunhead Grove, son of Charles Clements, gravedigger, and was the elder brother of James, who became Secretary to the London Cemetery Company. Henry was first employed as a gardener at Nunhead and served as sexton before being promoted to superintendent. He was buried at Nunhead.

The Chairman, Alexander Travers Hawes, remarked that the death of Henry Clements was a great loss to the Company. Indeed, he was the enterprising superintendent who had improved the general appearance of Nunhead by removing over one thousand old and decrepit gravestones and clearing away all the broken and unsightly ironwork.[6]

The vacancy thus created by Clements' death was filled by George

Henry Gillingham who had started work at Nunhead in 1888 as a boy gardener when he was just 15 years old, and afterwards spent many years as a gardener at Noirmont, Jersey, in the Channel Islands, where he met his future wife, Jessie Rouet. He returned to Nunhead as superintendent in 1916.[7]

George Henry Gillingham, appointed superintendent at Nunhead in 1916

In August 1916, the resignation through ill-health of the Secretary, Henry Martyn Dodd 'who had faithfully served the Company for 46 years' was considered a great loss to the Company, especially coming so soon after the death of the 'dutiful and hard-working' superintendent at Nunhead.

The death of Joseph Gurney Fowler FCA was also announced. A chartered accountant with the firm of Price, Waterhouse and Company, he was elected auditor to the London Cemetery Company in 1901, and remained in office until his death at Tonbridge, Kent, in 1916, aged 60. Also that year, Leonard Bonus, a director since 1904, died at the age of 59.

James Clements, the younger brother of the late superintendent at Nunhead, who was serving abroad with the army, was appointed Secretary 'in absentia' in the place of Dodd. Meanwhile, George Pole, a shareholder, was appointed Secretary 'pro tempore'.

Edward Day Boddington

Edward Day Boddington made several attempts to obtain a seat on the Board during 1917. At the General Meeting of Shareholders, which took place on the 13th February, a proposal was put to the members, three of whom voted in his favour and five against.

Another attempt to elect Boddington to the Board failed at the August meeting, despite the attendance of his wife and several supporters. The proposal was lost on a show of hands (the Chairman abstaining), by a majority of 16 votes against, to four votes in favour. It was announced that the directors had received proxies entitled to 1,716 votes against 431 in support of Boddington.

At the same meeting it was proposed by the Chairman, and seconded by Alfred Crawley, a shareholder, and carried by a majority of 16 members voting for, and five against, that the number of directors be kept at seven.

At the Special General Meeting held on the 10th December 1918, the Secretary read the notice and said the purpose of the meeting was to elect two shareholders as directors in the place of Robert Broadley (a director of 33 years) and George Louis Edward Raggett (a director of 17 years), both recently deceased. The Chairman went on to explain that under the Acts of Incorporation the number of directors should not be less than six, hence the reason for calling the meeting. A final attempt to elect Boddington to the Board was made, but the proposal was not seconded. William Cecil Harris MA, a lawyer of Caxton House, Westminster, was elected in the place of Broadley, and Horatio Gordon Hutchinson, a well-known golfer and author, was elected in the place of Raggett.

The reason for Boddington's unpopularity is unclear for he was a regular and vociferous attendant at meetings, and his once controversial proposal that a crematorium should be built in one of the Company's cemeteries was in due course adopted by the Board though not carried out due to the outbreak of war in 1914.

Boddington did not attend any meetings in 1919. He died at Brighton, Sussex, in 1920, aged 59. His death is noted in the *Register of Owners of Graves at Nunhead Cemetery* because he owned the burial rights to a grave in the cemetery but he is not buried there.

Between the two World Wars

Following the end of hostilities in 1918, the Company was registered under the Companies Acts of 1908/1917 as a Company limited by shares, and its name changed to the London Cemetery Company Limited. The capital of the Company was reduced from £99,576, consisting of 16,596 shares of £6 each, to £66,384, consisting of 16,596 shares of £4 each, and the sum of £2 per share, being capital in excess of the requirements of the Company, was returned to the shareholders.

In 1919 the Company had to cope with a large increase in staff wages, as well as carrying out essential repairs to all roads, paths, and buildings in their cemeteries. Also that year, the directors' remuneration was increased from £500 to £800 per annum.

James Clements, who was appointed Secretary 'in absentia' while on active service with the Royal Garrison Artillery in France, was demobilised in January 1919. He took up his post on returning to his home in Harlescott Road, Nunhead.

'Cross of Sacrifice' in Nunhead Cemetery sadly demolished in the1970s

In 1922, three large burial plots at Nunhead containing the graves of 580 servicemen and one servicewoman, who had died as a result of injuries received during active service in the First World War, were transferred to the Imperial War Graves Commission. A screen wall with bronze plaques and 'Cross of Sacrifice' were installed over the graves of the British servicemen buried in the largest plot. Elsewhere in the cemetery there are two small enclosed plots containing the graves of Australian, Canadian, New Zealand and South African servicemen.

Alexander Travers Hawes died in 1924, aged 73 years. He had been a director for 31 years and Chairman since 1907. Hawes, a magistrate and solicitor by profession, was a nephew of Sir Benjamin Hawes (1797-1862), a former Deputy Chairman of the London Cemetery Company. Hawes was succeeded by Henry Langton Stephenson.

Business carried on as usual throughout the 1920s, despite the opening of the Metropolitan Borough of Camberwell's 'New' Cemetery at nearby Honor Oak in 1927.[8]

Guardsmen attending the funeral of a colleague at Nunhead in the 1920s

In 1928, an exceptional sale of a piece of land at Highgate enabled the directors to recommend a bonus of two shillings (10p) per share in addition to the annual dividend of 5%, and in 1929 the sale of yet another large piece of land in Highgate Cemetery for the erection a new mausoleum, enabled the directors to pay a bonus of three shillings and sixpence (17.5p) in addition the usual dividend of 5%. The directors awarded themselves a bonus of £250 in recognition of the exceptional financial position of the Company.

Major General William Taylor Corrie (1838-1931) resigned from the Board in 1929 at the great age of 91, having served as a director for 41 years. He was brother-in-law to the late William Samuel Jones MA, JP (1831-1900), a former Chairman. His place on the Board was filled by Francis Richard Jones (d.1935).

The Company's share capital is reduced

At the Extraordinary General Meeting held on 10th February 1931, the capital of the Company was reduced to £33,192, consisting of 16,596 shares at £2 per share, and £2 per share was returned to the shareholders.

In 1932, Horatio Gordon Hutchinson, otherwise known as Horace Hutchinson, a well known golfer, all-round sportsman and author, who had served on the Board since 1918, died at the age of 73. His family had long been connected with the London Cemetery Company: his father, General William Nelson Hutchinson, was a director, and his grandfather, the Revd Dr Russell, was the Company's first Chairman.

The death of Maurice Chapman Anderson, who had been a member of the Board for 36 years, was announced in 1933. He was 82 years old.

In 1933 the Governor of the Bank of England purchased two vaults and one ante-room on the southern wing of the Eastern Catacomb at Nunhead, and one vault and one ante-room on the northern wing of the Eastern Catacomb. These had remained unoccupied since being constructed in 1840 and were required to receive the exhumed human remains from the garden of the Bank of England, the former churchyard of St Christopher-le-Stocks. Between the 26th July and 8th November 1933, 74 cases of human remains and 12 lead coffins were transferred to Nunhead Cemetery. The remaining 11 cases of human remains were removed from the former churchyard on the 1st December 1933 and placed in the one of the ante-rooms and the entrance to the room was sealed. A lead coffin brought to Nunhead at the same time is believed to have contained the remains of William Daniel Jenkins (1767-1798), a bank clerk, who was known as 'Long Jenkins' due to his extraordinary height of almost seven feet. His body had been buried in the grounds of the Bank of England to keep it safe from the body-snatchers and anatomists. The crypt of St Christopher's Church was cleared as early as 1867 and the human remains placed in the Eastern Catacomb.

Leonard Eustace Croker was appointed to the Board on the 12th February 1935. His name disappears from the Company's Minutes in 1939.

In 1936 Herbert Hardwick Trist resigned from the Board having been a director for over 50 years. Lord Courtown (James Richard Neville Stopford) OBE, DL, JP, was appointed in his place. A grandson of Richard Cornwallis Neville FSA, 4th Baron Braybrooke (1820-61), Lord Courtown had served in the South African War and First World War, and was Mayor of Aylesbury in 1927-8. He succeeded his father as the 7th Earl of Courtown in 1933, and was Deputy Assistant Adjutant General at the War Office during the Second World War.

Amédée Mercier, the son of a stockbroker, was appointed to the Board on the 11th February 1936. His appointment was tragically short however, for he died at Croydon later that year, aged 46. His place was filled by

Major H. S. Armstrong who was appointed a director on the 9th February 1937.

The Company's business remained constant between the two World Wars. Common burials continued to be the mainstay at Nunhead Cemetery throughout the 1920s and 1930s. The total number of burials at Nunhead in 1937 was 1,790 of which 1,148 were in common graves.

The Second World War

At the General Meeting held on 13th February 1940, Lord Courtown was called to the Chair and regretted to announce the death of Henry Langton Stephenson, who had been Chairman for the last 15 years. Stephenson, a stockbroker, had served on the Board for over 30 years. At the same meeting the Board agreed to transfer the Company's Head Office from 29 New Bridge Street to Nunhead Cemetery for the duration of the war.

At the General Meeting which took place on the 11th February 1941, the new Chairman, Lord Courtown, remarked at the considerable amount of bomb damage suffered in the Company's cemeteries. He expressed his warmest thanks to all those members of staff who had carried out their duties in an 'exemplary manner' under the most trying conditions.

Gravediggers in Nunhead Cemetery during the Second World War

Several bombs fell in Nunhead Cemetery during the blitz on London in 1940 and 1941. A large mausoleum, belonging to the Harris family of Gorringe Park, Mitcham, and a lime tree on the west side of the main walk leading from the entrance gates up to the Anglican chapel, were demolished and many private vaults and monuments were destroyed or badly damaged by blast. A bomb fell in the East Crescent leaving a deep crater and damaging several substantial monuments, while another destroyed part of the boundary wall fronting Linden Grove causing much damage to graves and scattering human remains into the public road. The Eastern Catacomb was damaged and the Dissenters' chapel suffered irreparable damage later in the war.

At Highgate a bomb exploded close to the Terrace Catacombs in the West Cemetery causing extensive damage and leaving a huge crater some 20ft deep by 50ft wide.[9]

Nunhead's superintendent resigns

The East Gate Lodge (superintendent's house) at Nunhead was badly damaged during an air-raid and rendered uninhabitable for a time. The superintendent, George Henry Gillingham and his wife, moved out of the cemetery much to the consternation of the Chairman who wanted them to return to the lodge when the necessary repairs had been carried out.

The superintendent had no desire to return to live in the cemetery. He made it perfectly clear in a courteous letter to Lord Courtown, that under no circumstances would he and his wife wish to return to the lodge. He would, however, continue to give his 'best and whole attention' to the management of the cemetery and had arranged for three men to attend the cemetery every night for fire watching and other duties. The directors, however, were not satisfied with this arrangement and asked Gillingham to resign. On relinquishing his post in June 1941, he was presented with a gift of £150 in recognition of his 'long and honourable' service. After his resignation the duties of superintendent were carried out by Hewitt and Pearce, clerks.

Although the shareholders continued to meet at the Company's former Head Office in the City of London, the Company was run throughout the war years from Nunhead Cemetery. In the summer of 1942, however, the Head Office was vacated completely, thereby saving the Company around £350 per annum.

The death of William Cecil Harris, director, was announced in 1942.

His son, Major William Barclay Harris, was appointed a director 'in absentia' while serving abroad with HM forces.

Only half the usual Dividend could be paid in 1942. Lord Courtown blamed the high wages and excessive taxes, and claimed that business was poor because so many families had been evacuated from London. He pointed out that the other London cemetery companies had also cut their dividends.

Also in 1942, the cast-iron boundary railings and decorative metal on most of the monuments in Nunhead Cemetery were removed by order of Camberwell Borough Council on behalf of the Government. The scrap metal was supposed to help with the war effort. Interestingly, the council's own cemeteries at nearby Brenchley Gardens and Forest Hill Road retained most of their railings and metal work.

The boundary railings at Highgate were also scheduled for removal, but following correspondence between the London Cemetery Company Ltd and St Pancras Borough Council, they were allowed to remain.

During the 'little blitz' on southeast London in March 1944, several bombs fell in the centre of Nunhead Cemetery and along the east path, causing extensive damage to burial vaults and graves.

In August 1944, the second mass wartime evacuation of mothers and children was under way as Germany intensified its attacks on London with its new secret weapon, the V1 flying bomb. Several flying bombs, or doodlebugs as Londoners called them, fell in the vicinity of Nunhead Cemetery. One caused serious damage to the cemetery and dozens of graves when it came down and destroyed several houses in Ivydale Road.

The Revd Canon George Potter (d.1960), known as Father Potter of Peckham, and his colleague, Father Francis Williams, both of the Brotherhood of the Holy Cross, shared chaplain's duty at Nunhead Cemetery for about three years during the war, and claimed to have buried about 3,000 air-raid victims between them. Father Potter notes in his memoirs that over 50 bombs fell in the cemetery and a chapel and dozens of large monuments were destroyed.[10]

At the General Meeting held at 29 New Bridge Street on 22nd February 1945, Lord Courtown remarked that Major William Barclay Harris, a director, was still serving abroad with the army on active service. He also paid a 'high tribute' to all the members of staff who had kept the cemeteries in such a satisfactory condition despite the many difficulties caused by the war.

75

Post-war woes

After the war the Company was in severe financial difficulties. Major William Barclay Harris, who had been appointed to the Board 'in absentia', attended his first General Meeting on the 19th February 1946.

At the General Meeting held at 29 New Bridge Street on 22nd April 1947, Lord Courtown informed the shareholders that Frank Steane Price, 'auditor for many years' had resigned, and Walter Edmund Parker had been appointed in his place. Both gentlemen were partners in the firm of Price, Waterhouse and Company. Frank Steane Price had served the Company as auditor since the First World War, and Sir Walter Edmund Parker (1908-81) - he was knighted in 1974 - was Chief Accountant at the Board of Trade in 1940, and Assistant Secretary to the Board of Trade in 1941. He served as auditor to the Duchy of Cornwall from 1957, and became President of the Institute of Chartered Accountants in 1967.

On Monday, 22nd March 1948, the shareholders met at their former Head Office, 29 New Bridge Street, for the very last time, and the building was sold. Ordinary profit was not enough to pay a dividend but, as a good profit had been made on the redemption and sale of stocks, the Board felt justified in recommending the usual dividend of five per cent.

Lord Courtown proposed that the directors' remuneration be increased to £1,430 per annum, less tax, and this was seconded by Mr Hewitt, Head Clerk, and carried unanimously. It was also resolved that 'the directors' may grant special remuneration to any member of the Board, who, on being called upon, shall being willing to render special or extra services to the Company. Such special remuneration may be made payable by a lump sum, by a way of salary, by a percentage or profits, or by any or all of these methods.

As late as 1949, 12 full-time and one part-time staff were employed at Nunhead, including a clerk, a foreman, seven gardeners/gravediggers, one groundsman, a handyman, and two gatekeepers, one of whom was part-time. The highest paid member of staff was the foreman who received £5.12.6d (£5.62½p) per week. The total weekly wage bill for Nunhead Cemetery was £61.[11]

Shareholders meet at Nunhead Cemetery

The first General Meeting of Shareholders to be held at Nunhead Cemetery took place on 5th April 1949. Just six persons were present: Lord

Courtown and three directors, viz: Messrs Harris, Hilleary and Rawlins. Also in attendance were Head Clerk Hewitt, and Highgate's superintendent, F. R. Channon. Hugh Graham Gregory, a director, was out of the country.

At the General Meeting held at Nunhead Cemetery on 5th April 1950 six persons were in attendance, including the Chairman and Messrs Gregory, Harris and Rawlins, directors. Messrs Hewitt and Channon were also present. Hugh Graham Gregory proposed that 'Lord Courtown who is 72 and retiring from the Board by rotation under the Articles of Association' be re-elected a director of the Company. This was seconded by Mr Rawlins and carried unanimously.

An Extraordinary General Meeting was held at St Bride's Institute, London, EC, on the 23rd January 1951 and was attended by Lord Courtown in the chair, Messrs Harris and Hillerary, directors, several shareholders in person, and the proxies of 43 shareholders. It was resolved that the issued capital of the Company be reduced from £33,192, consisting of 16,596 shares of £2 each, to £16,596, consisting of 16,596 shares of £1 each, and that £1 per share should be returned to shareholders. The Company reserved the right to raise further capital to the extent of £20,000 by issuing further shares as conferred by Section 6 of the London Cemetery Company Act 1911. At the same meeting the number of directors was reduced from four to three.

From 1st May 1951 to 2nd April 1957 inclusive, General Meetings were held annually at the offices of Messrs Smallfield and Rawlins, Chartered Accountants, Cannon Street, London, EC. Two of the partners were also directors of the London Cemetery Company Ltd.

It was reported that the church and conservatory boilers at Highgate were worn out, and Edward Hilleary had succeeded in acquiring two second-hand boilers as suitable replacements.

Also at Highgate, the Company was involved in litigation over a dead elm tree which had been growing on the Cundey grave in the Eastern Cemetery. The tree, on grave number 25067, square 81, had come down during a storm causing extensive damage to adjacent gravestones. Acting on the advice of their solicitor, the Board decided to proceed with legal action against the owners of the grave. The case occupied two days, and the judgement of the court was against the Company. It was held that the grant of an exclusive right of burial is strictly limited to the terms of the grant itself, and in no case can it divest the cemetery authority of their responsibilities as owners of the land. The court's decision was bad news for the Company because they were presented with a £582 bill.[12]

In May 1952 an architect and war damage officials visited Nunhead Cemetery and repairs were later carried out to the road fronting the Anglican chapel, the Eastern Catacomb, and the boundary wall fronting Linden Grove. The bomb-ruined Dissenters' chapel was demolished and the contents of the crypt placed in the vaults of the Anglican chapel. Bomb-damaged monuments, of which there were many dotted around the cemetery, were not repaired as they belonged to the owners of the graves. The Company's policy was to encourage bramble and ivy growth on damaged memorials in an attempt to screen them from public view.

In the summer of 1952 the Karl Marx Library contacted the Board about erecting a new monument to Karl Marx in Highgate's East Cemetery. A deal was struck and the remains of the Marx family were exhumed on the 22nd September 1954 and reburied in a new grave in square 94. The Board charged £2,000 for the new grave plot, but even this sizeable sum was insufficient to help cover the ever increasing costs in running the cemeteries.

The Head Clerk, Mr Hewitt, resigned in September 1952. The Chairman thanked him for his long service and the Board presented him with an ex-gratia payment of 200 guineas.

In 1953, to meet a rise of five shillings (25p) a week awarded to gravediggers, the charges for common interments at Nunhead were increased by five shillings (25p), and a charge of 10 shillings (50p) was introduced for the privilege of placing a small memorial, no greater than 12 inches high and 12 inches wide, on common graves.

The Chairman and three directors attended an Extraordinary General Meeting held at the offices of Smallfield, Rawlins and Company on 1st April 1954, at which it was resolved to reduce the issued capital of the Company from 16,596 shares at £1 each to 16,596 shares at five shillings (25p) each. Between 1911 and 1954 the issued capital of the Company had been reduced from £132,768 to just £4,149.

At the Meeting of the Board which took place at Nunhead Cemetery on the 9th February 1954, 'warm congratulations and good wishes for the future' were expressed to the Secretary, James Clements, who had joined the Company 64 years ago that very day.

James Clements resigned as Secretary in July 1955 and was appointed Consultant to the Company for three years at a fee of £300 per annum. The Board resolved that Albert Edward Pearce be appointed Secretary in his place. Mr Pearce, it was noted, was well-qualified to the post for he had been Head Clerk and had carried on the superintendent's duties at Nunhead during the Second World War.

The death of former director Hugh Graham Gregory at the end of 1955 was announced. He was 76. A partner in the firm of Gully, Ross, Stephens and Gregory, Chartered Accountants, of 1 Broad Street Place, London, he had been a director of the London Cemetery Company Ltd for 17 years until resigning from the Board in February 1951.

At the Meeting of the Board held at Nunhead on the 15th November 1955, Barney Pike, a shareholder, stated that in view of his large holding in the Company he would like to become a director. He was invited to join the Board in January 1956.

James Clements, Secretary,
London Cemetery Company 1917-1955

Ernest Brackley died in 1956, aged 76. He was for more than 40 years the uniformed gatekeeper at Nunhead Cemetery. He resided at 127 Linden Grove, virtually opposite the cemetery gates, and was buried at Nunhead.[13]

In February 1956, the Labour MP, Captain Henry Kerby MP (1914-1971), offered his services to the Board as interpreter on the forthcoming visit of USSR leaders to see the new Karl Marx monument at Highgate. On the night of 16th April 1956, however, the monument was attacked by vandals and daubed with red paint. The superintendent, at the request of the police, succeeded in removing the paint before the visiting Russian dignitaries arrived in the country.[14]

79

A final attempt to build a crematorium at Nunhead fails

Honor Oak Crematorium, opened by Camberwell Borough Council at the start of the Second World War, attracted a lot of business away from Nunhead Cemetery and once again the Board discussed building a crematorium at Nunhead.

At the next meeting of the directors which took place at Nunhead Cemetery in September 1956, the Secretary produced letters from the Bishop of Woolwich, the Medical Officer of Health for Camberwell Borough Council, and the Company's solicitor, in reply to an enquiry about the possibility of constructing a crematorium in Nunhead Cemetery. Hav-

ing carefully considered the contents of the letters, the Chairman regretted to inform the Board that under the Cremation Act 1902 a crematorium could not be erected on consecrated ground. As there were no unconsecrated plots large enough in any of the Company's cemeteries, the scheme, first put forward by Edward Day Boddington as early as 1898, was finally laid to rest.

Ernest Brackley
Gatekeeper at Nunhead Cemetery (see page 79)

80

5: THE DEMISE OF THE LONDON CEMETERY COMPANY AND CLOSURE OF NUNHEAD CEMETERY

In 1956, the nursery, greenhouses and stables at Nunhead were abandoned and the last surviving donkey was disposed of. The directors sold the Townshend Yard Nursery at Highgate for £3,000, and the sale of the superintendent's lodge, also at Highgate, raised a further £2,750.

Inside one of the abandoned greenhouses at Nunhead Cemetery

In September 1956, somewhat surprisingly in view of the Company's continuing financial problems, electric lighting was installed in both gate lodges at Nunhead. Further expense was incurred when the pinnacles on the roof of the Anglican chapel at Nunhead were found to be in a dangerous condition and had to be taken down. The castellated parapet above the carriage porch was removed at the same time.

At the Meeting of the Board held at Nunhead Cemetery on 1st November 1956, Edward Kenneth Macleod Hilleary, a director, informed his colleagues that a solicitor had written to members offering them, on behalf of their clients, eight shillings and sixpence (42½p) per share. Having carefully considered the matter, the Board decided to write to all shareholders and recommend that they should refuse the offer.

At the next Board Meeting, which took place at Nunhead on 18th December 1956, Barney Pike reported having seen an advertisement in the *Financial Times* offering for sale a block of shares in the Company. He believed the advertisement was not in the interests of the Company, and had therefore acquired the entire block of 931 shares at nine shillings (45p) per share to prevent the advertisement continuing. He felt the advertisement was a direct result of the directors' letter to shareholders.[1]

The death of the Earl of Courtown

The death of Lord Courtown on the 26th January 1957, at the age of 79, hastened the end of the London Cemetery Company Ltd. Barney Pike became Chairman and the directors considered handing over Highgate Cemetery to the Metropolitan Borough of St Pancras. The new Chairman personally approached St Pancras Council with the Board's proposals but the offer was turned down. The Chairman also visited the Soviet Consulate in London with the Board's recommendation that the remains of Karl Marx should be removed from Highgate's East Cemetery and taken to the Soviet Union for re-interment there. The Soviet Consulate dismissed the Board's suggestion without consideration.

Major Harris tendered his resignation from the Board in June 1957 due to pressure of work. Another two directors, Edward Kenneth Macleod Hilleary and Robert Collet, both resigned from the Board in July 1957. Edward Hilleary had been a director since 1940, and Robert Collet, a chartered accountant with the firm of Smallfield, Rawlins & Co, of Cannon Street, London, EC4, had been a director since March 1950. Their places were filled by Alexander Fines and Leslie Melville. Melville resigned from the Board after just six months in January 1958.

At the Extraordinary General Meeting held at Nunhead Cemetery on Tuesday 11th February 1958, Barney Pike, Chairman, and Albert Edward Pearce, director and Secretary, were joined by Mrs R. Pike, Mr J. M. Pike, and Mr J. David. The Secretary read the notice convening the meeting and the Chairman proposed a Special Resolution, the basis of which was to sell, lease, or otherwise dispose of the whole or any part of the estates or other property of the Company, and to create, sell and deal in freehold and leasehold ground rents, and generally to deal in, or with, any land and house property and any other property, whether real or personal, and to acquire and hold shares in any other company having objects similar to those of the London Cemetery Company Ltd. This was seconded by Mr J. David and carried unanimously.

The London Cemetery Company Ltd acquires Rosebank Cemetery

The Extraordinary General Meeting held at Nunhead Cemetery on Tuesday 15th April 1958, was attended by Barney Pike, Albert Pearce, Mrs R. Pike, Mr J. M. Pike, and Mrs G. David (on behalf of Mr J. David). The Chairman proposed the following Special Resolution: that the Company as forthwith acquire all the issued Share Capital of Raybar Properties Ltd for £28,500. This was seconded by Mrs G. David and carried unanimously.

Later that year the Chairman visited Edinburgh and shares in several cemeteries were acquired. The grounds of Rosebank Cemetery, Edinburgh, were transferred to the London Cemetery Company Ltd by the Edinburgh and Leith Cemetery Company Ltd, and the 16,596 ordinary shares of five shillings (25p) each, were converted to non-voting ordinary shares.

The last General Meeting of the London Cemetery Company Ltd took place at Nunhead Cemetery on the 14th July 1959.

By January 1960, Nunhead, Highgate and Rosebank cemeteries had been incorporated as United Cemeteries Ltd, a subsidiary of Raybar Holdings Ltd, and the London Cemetery Company Ltd ceased to exist.

The closure of Nunhead Cemetery

The deteriorating condition of Nunhead Cemetery had been a cause of concern to Camberwell Borough Council for several years. In 1963 it was the subject of a joint meeting between representatives of the Metropolitan Boroughs of Camberwell, Bermondsey, and Southwark, and they agreed to defer consideration of the 'problem of Nunhead Cemetery' until all three boroughs had been amalgamated to form a new single local authority - the London Borough of Southwark - which was due to take effect in 1965.

In trying to tackle the problems of Nunhead Cemetery, the Council of the newly created London Borough of Southwark faced several legal difficulties, for example the London Cemetery Company Act of 1836 prevented the local authority, and anyone else for that matter, from buying the cemetery and, as there were insufficient funds available in respect of that cemetery, the Council was unable to compel the owners, United Cemeteries Ltd, to keep the cemetery in good repair. Furthermore, the Council's opinion was that the owners were not obliged to use the income generated at Highgate Cemetery for maintenance at Nunhead.

United Cemeteries Limited became a wholly owned subsidiary of the Raybourne Group Ltd in 1968, the latter being the successor to Raybar Holdings Ltd under a change of name registered at Companies House. In the autumn of that year, the owners decided they could no longer run Nunhead Cemetery on an economical basis as the cost of maintaining the cemetery was far more than the income raised from burials. Indeed, the burial rights to only eight graves were sold that year. The very last grave was numbered 44,760.

From the opening of the cemetery in July 1840 to its closure on the 31st December 1968, there had been 223,936 interments in the consecrated ground and 45,812 in the unconsecrated ground amounting to a total of 269,748 burials. Some private graves were purchased but never used, while others contained just a single body. The majority of burials at Nunhead were in common graves, generally, but not always, placed near the boundary walls. Some areas of the cemetery are very heavily buried, for example square 13 contains upwards of 10,000 bodies in 750, mostly common, graves.

Common graves were often reused. At Nunhead, for example, in 1855 eight bodies were buried in grave number 3768, square 132, and another two bodies were buried in the same grave one year later. The grave

A common grave in Nunhead Cemetery

84

was reopened in 1866 to receive another body, and in 1925 a further five coffins were placed in the grave. Common grave number 3769, square 34, at Nunhead, contains 18 bodies, seven of which were buried in 1855 followed by another six in 1918, and five more in 1952.

No less than 31 bodies were interred in grave number 4364. This grave was first opened in 1856, reopened in 1918, and again in 1952. Grave number 6762, square 22, contains 23 bodies. The first ten were buried in 1861, followed by eight more in 1919, and another five in 1955, by which time grave space was at a premium and any unused space was being utilised for burials.

Access to graves denied

In January 1969, United Cemeteries Ltd gave notice that Nunhead Cemetery would be closed, no more graves would be sold and no further maintenance would be undertaken. The gates were padlocked and access to graves, including those only recently purchased, was denied.

Burials in existing private graves were permitted for a short while but, as ground staff were no longer employed at the cemetery, funeral directors had to make their own arrangements to open and close graves on behalf of their clients. Several burials took place without the Company's knowledge and, as a result, these 'unofficial' interments were not recorded in the cemetery ledgers.

According to Southwark Council's solicitors, section 1 of the 1853 Burials Act (which provides for an Order in Council for the discontinuance of interments in a burial ground) did not apply to cemeteries established under private Acts of Parliament, and the 1836 Act incorporating the London Cemetery Company made no provision for the permanent closure of any of its cemeteries, therefore, Nunhead Cemetery had been closed by its owners without legal authority.

Burial Registers and other records stored in the lodges at Nunhead, including some relating to Highgate Cemetery, were removed to Monkey Island Hotel, near Maidenhead, the new headquarters of United Cemeteries Ltd. The hotel secretary complained to newspaper reporters that she was expected to deal with dozens of enquiries about the closure of Nunhead Cemetery, as well as trying to do her usual job of attending to hotel reservations.[2]

In 1970, residents, grave owners and local clergymen, were outraged when United Cemeteries Ltd allowed a movie to be filmed in Nunhead

Cemetery. The offending scenes, for a feature film called 'Melody', included a 12-year-old Mark Lester (later of 'Oliver' fame) running amok among gravestones and being kissed by child actress Tracy Hyde. The cemetery company charged the movie makers £10 a day for filming in the cemetery.[3]

The closure of the cemetery forced several local stonemasons to shut up shop too. Some firms, such as Henry Daniel and Co, had been operating in Nunhead since the establishment of the cemetery in 1840, and only ceased business due to the closure of the cemetery.

Staff outside the premises of Henry Daniel & Co, Linden Grove c.1945

Second from the left is Jack Brackley, a letter cutter/engraver, son of Ernest Brackley, cemetery gatekeeper. On the far right is Mr Lee, the proprietor

The campaign to reopen Nunhead Cemetery gathers momentum

Disgruntled residents and grave owners, led by the Revd Percy Gray of St Crispin's Church, Bermondsey, and Bob Mellish MP (later Baron Mellish of Bermondsey), eventually succeeded in persuading United Cemeteries Ltd to open the cemetery to grave owners and visitors at weekends.

The Revd Percy Gray organised all night vigils outside the cemetery gates in Linden Grove, held several protest meetings and helped raise a petition calling on Southwark Council to take over, restore, and reopen the cemetery on a permanent basis. Meanwhile, the Bishop of Southwark led a deputation of disconcerted funeral directors to Southwark Town Hall, and the Commonwealth War Graves Commission expressed their concern at the 'wild condition' of the cemetery which made it difficult for staff to maintain the war grave plots to their 'usual high standards'.

Southwark Council's view was that, because the cemetery affected people throughout London and well beyond, its improvement should be treated as a regional matter. The Government and the Greater London Council, on the other hand, disagreed claiming it was entirely a matter for the local authority to deal with.

In October 1970, it was reported that Chingford Mount Cemetery had put in a bid to United Cemeteries Ltd to take over Nunhead Cemetery, but nothing came of the offer.[4]

The author, photographer and broadcaster, Lucinda Lambton, visited Nunhead Cemetery in 1972 while 'combing' Britain for reminders of the Victorian age. Her aim was to compile a personal anthology that might provoke others into taking greater care of national treasures at risk through neglect. She was appalled at the dereliction around her, and while trudging through 'the thickly-wooded land where foxes and rabbits can be seen in a particularly dismal part of South London.....and almost every grave has been prised open', she found herself entirely alone, for not one other person was there from the 'grim and overcrowded' surrounding area.[5]

The Raybourne Group Ltd's proposals for Nunhead Cemetery

In October 1972 Southwark Council's Highway and Works Committee asked the Raybourne Group Ltd if they were prepared to sell Nunhead Cemetery to the Council, if it could be arranged, and if so on what terms. The Raybourne Group Ltd ignored the Council's enquiry and instead submitted proposals, prepared by their architects, for the redevelopment of a section of the cemetery in collaboration with Southwark Council.

The Raybourne Group's plans were for an area of approximately 13 acres, said to have been less heavily used for burials than the remainder, upon which it was proposed to construct a communal building and high-rise blocks of flats to provide hostel accommodation for up to 1,200 students. Very few graves would be disturbed, they claimed, as it was proposed to build the flats on stilts thus leaving the graves under the buildings. Additionally, an area of about eight acres around the proposed development would be laid out as a 'memorial park', and the remaining 30 acres or so would be left as a 'controlled wilderness'. All human remains disturbed by the building work would be re-interred in a new 'Avenue of Remembrance'.

After careful consideration Southwark Council came to the conclusion that the proposals were unacceptable for a number of reasons, including the proposed zoning of the land as 'metropolitan open space' by the Greater London Council, public opposition to the plans, and the uncertainty of the Council's financial liability.[6]

Despite turning down the Raybourne Group's extraordinary proposals, the equally bizarre possibility of using some of the burial land for social housing was being investigated by Southwark Council. The proposed housing scheme was eventually abandoned, mainly due to the high costs involved and the added problem of re-burying or cremating over 5,000 bodies per acre.[7]

In reply to further approaches by Southwark

Desecrated mausoleum in Nunhead Cemetery c.1972

Council, representatives of the Raybourne Group Ltd said they would be prepared to dispose of Nunhead Cemetery to the Council 'subject to a mutually satisfactory price being negotiated and subject to contract'. The Raybourne Group Ltd were also anxious to dispose of Highgate Cemetery to Camden Council, but their offer was turned down.

Within a few years of its closure Nunhead Cemetery had become an uncontrolled wilderness.[8] Gravestones disappeared in the undergrowth and the vandals and grave robbers moved in. A First World War memorial, maintained by the Commonwealth War Graves Commission, was desecrated, and dozens of bronze plaques commemorating hundreds of British soldiers buried in the cemetery were stolen. The Anglican chapel was set ablaze and both gate lodges were broken into and valuable records destroyed. The Eastern Catacomb was raided and coffins dragged from their compartments, prised open and dashed to pieces. Charred documents and human remains littered the cemetery's roads and pathways, and the site became a favourite dumping ground for illegal fly tipping.[9]

While the future of the cemetery was being debated by Southwark Council and the Raybourne Group Ltd, grave owners and local people fed up with the state of the place, went into action with scythes and spades. Prompted by the Revd Percy Gray, residents, students, and other volunteers went to work cutting back undergrowth and clearing paths. Biology students at King's College Hospital, led by Martin Heath, patrolled the cemetery in an attempt to stop vandalism, and local Scouts promised to carry out work in the cemetery with the approval of its owners.[10]

Nunhead Cemetery is discussed at the House of Commons

On Tuesday 26th March 1974 a meeting about the future of Nunhead Cemetery took place at the House of Commons. Those attending included Gordon James Oakes MP (1931-2005), Parliamentary Under Secretary for the Department of the Environment; Bob Mellish (1913-1998), MP for Bermondsey, later Baron Mellish, who led a deputation of his constituents; Mrs O'Shea, representing the Nunhead Action Group (NAG); Southwark Council's Borough Engineer and Deputy Town Clerk; Alderman Allen and Councillor Jones of Southwark Council, and several officers of the Department of the Environment.[11]

Bob Mellish explained to the Minister the degree of distress that had been caused by the neglected condition and closure of Nunhead Cemetery, especially to those with relatives buried there.

Mrs O'Shea, representing NAG, said her group had been advised that the cemetery had great potential as a nature reserve in its present condition, and it already had a wide variety of birds, animals and plants. The Bermondsey deputation, however, were in favour of the land being retained and used only as a working cemetery.

A compromise was suggested, and the possibility of the land being used as an open space, with a limited number of private graves still in use, was discussed. It was not considered necessary to deconsecrate the land provided the use was not incompatible with consecration.

The legal difficulties resulting from the London Cemetery Company Act of 1836 which prohibited the sale of the cemetery were discussed, and the Minister promised early legislation to resolve this particular problem, possibly by means of a 'back of the chair' Bill. In any event, it was agreed by all concerned that the 'problem' of Nunhead Cemetery had continued long enough and had to be resolved.

It was decided that in order to overcome the problem, it was necessary to obtain another Act of Parliament which Southwark Council would promote by means of the Greater London Council (General Powers) Bill to be placed before Parliament in the 1974-75 session. The Bill would enable the Council to buy the cemetery compulsorily and, if successful, the Council would retain part of the site (about 12 acres) as a burial ground, and preserve the remainder (about 30 acres) as a public open space and nature reserve.

Southwark Council had received a report on the wildlife and vegetation in the cemetery and were impressed by its potential as an educational asset for parties of schoolchildren, with opportunities of laying out nature trails.

The burial area would be gradually converted to a lawn cemetery with tombstones being laid flat, covered, and if desired by relatives, replaced by marker stones. It was proposed to seek powers in the Bill to extinguish burial rights in old private graves in which there had been no burials for at least 75 years, so that they could be used for further burials.[12] Somewhat surprisingly, the architectural and historical aspects of the cemetery were not considered nor discussed.

Southwark Council takes control of Nunhead Cemetery

The Bill authorising Southwark Council to compulsorily purchase the cemetery and its buildings became law on the 7th August 1975, and the Council took possession on the 24th November 1975 for the nominal sum of £1 plus undisclosed costs.[13]

In the meantime the vandalism and desecration at Nunhead Cemetery continued. In October 1975 a Balham man was remanded on bail accused of unlawfully removing the head of a corpse from the cemetery. The head,

*Walls and piers at the Linden Grove entrance to Nunhead Cemetery being
dismantled and reconstructed in January 1976*

which was found in a pond on Wandsworth Common, was later identified
as that of a woman who had been buried at Nunhead just six months earlier.[14]

On taking possession of the cemetery, Southwark Council immediately
set about making it safe. A 'Working Party' was set up under the chair-
manship of Anthony Wragg, Deputy Borough Engineer, which comprised
officers from several Council Departments. Their first priority was to protect life and limb, and remove tons of fly-tipped waste from the entrances
and roads. The mile long boundary wall was repaired and a new chain
link fence erected. Over 500 dangerous trees (mostly diseased and dead
elms) were felled, and the Eastern Catacomb, vandalised brick graves and
private vaults sealed, made safe and secure, or else demolished. The un-
stable Portland stone gate piers at the Linden Grove entrance were dismantled and reinstalled in January 1976.

Nature Conservancy Council officers were consulted by the Council
and made three visits to the site. They emphasised the importance, before
any clearance work was undertaken, of preparing a management plan both
for the burial and open space sections, and this was undertaken by Southwark Council's landscape architects.[15]

Clearance work carried out at Nunhead using unskilled labour

At the meeting of the Conservation Areas Advisory Committee, held at Southwark Town Hall on 28th March 1977, the Borough Planner reported that heavy clearance work associated with creating the 'lawn cemetery' at Nunhead had been undertaken in a 'crash programme' using unskilled labour. It was thought that the 'lawn cemetery' would continue to be used for interment for the next 40 years. He went on to say that vandalism had rendered the chapel unserviceable for use by funeral parties, but could be used as an interpretative centre with botanical and biological display panels and exhibitions of wildlife, etc. It was also suggested that the roof could be reconstructed with a viewing platform looking out over the cemetery and towards central London. It was also claimed that the woodland area had great potential to become an 'unsurpassed educational asset' for the schools and colleges of south London. The open areas and their facilities should be clearly signposted from the entrances as in Forestry Commission and Country Park amenity areas.

Undergrowth was removed and 'dense sycamore forests' were thinned by 45 young men employed under the Manpower Commission's Job Creation Scheme. The clearance work was supervised by Arthur Vercouttere, who had the onerous task of managing up to 20 youths at a time, while continuing to carry out his duties as superintendent of Southwark's three cemeteries and crematorium. Needless to say, new tools went missing, important monuments were damaged by careless clearance work, and several specimen trees were destroyed or damaged by bonfires.

Southwark's elected members were anxious not to do anything which might be regarded as incompatible with use of the land as a cemetery. It was, therefore, proposed to leave a large section untouched as a nature reserve and to lay out a small area as a place for quiet recreation.[16]

By the end of August 1977 over £120,000 had been spent in carrying out essential works. It was estimated that the total cost of clearance work and restoration would take at least eight years at a cost of £600,000.

New burials commence at Nunhead

A section on the southern side of Nunhead Cemetery was set aside for new burials. Old monuments and headstones were removed and broken up, and intermediate burials between existing graves commenced in November 1979.

Among the first interments in the newly prepared ground was that of Field Marshal Sir William Maynard Gomm (1784-1875), Lord of the Manor of Rotherhithe and hero of Waterloo, whose body was exhumed from the demolished church of Christ Church, Rotherhithe, and reburied at Nunhead on the 26th November 1979. Between the 7th November 1979 and the end of March 1983, over 930 interments had taken place in the cleared area.[17]

Highgate Cemetery's new friends

In north London, the Council of the London Borough of Camden had been given powers to compulsorily purchase Highgate Cemetery from the Raybourne Group Ltd by means of the GLC (General Powers) Bill of 1975 - the same Bill that had empowered Southwark Council to compulsorily purchase Nunhead Cemetery. Camden Council, however, declined to do so. The Friends of Highgate Cemetery (FOHC), a voluntary conservation group which had been set up in 1975,[18] succeeded in securing several deletions and amendments to the Bill and, had Camden Council taken on the responsibility of running the cemetery, they were bound by law to consult with a body representing national or local opinion before carrying out any work in the cemetery, including the removal of human remains and monuments. These conditions may have influenced Camden Council's decision not to take over the cemetery.

The Highgate Cemetery Trust, a registered charity, was set up and in 1981 two members of FOHC formed a company called Pinemarsh Ltd, and acquired the freehold of the cemetery from the Raybourne Group Ltd for the nominal sum of £50.[19]

In 1983 the Historic Buildings Council declared Highgate Cemetery a place of outstanding historic and architectural interest and a company, Highgate Cemetery Ltd, was created to supervise the work of the Manpower Services Commission.

In 1988 the freehold of Highgate Cemetery was transferred to a new organisation, the Highgate Cemetery Charity, which immediately transferred the freehold to the Official Custodian of Charities in order to secure the future of the cemetery as a burial ground and as a place of historic importance forever.[20]

6: NUNHEAD 'S NEW FRIENDS

The sad neglect of Nunhead Cemetery by its former owners, and the vandalism which had worsened since Southwark Council had taken possession in November 1975, had left the cemetery in a sorry state. The mile long boundary wall had been repaired, hundreds of dead trees had been felled - regrettably damaging or destroying many fine monuments in the process - and dangerous gravestones had been 'made safe' by demolishing them. But, despite these so-called 'improvements', the general appearance of the cemetery continued to resemble a rubbish tip.

In October 1978, the late George Taylor, Secretary of the Southwark Branch of the National Union of Public Employees (NUPE), wrote to the present writer, who was then Chairman of the Peckham Society (the amenity society for London SE15), expressing his concern at the deplorable state of Nunhead Cemetery and inviting him to chair a meeting of interested parties at Southwark Town Hall. George Taylor proposed forming a pressure group of interested parties, similar to that set up at Highgate three years earlier, to be called 'The Friends of Nunhead Cemetery', details of which appeared in a letter written by him and published in the *South London Press.*[1]

Disappointingly, despite support from the Peckham Society and the Nunhead Residents' Association, there was little or no response from other groups or the public in general, therefore nothing came of this first attempt to form a conservation group for Nunhead Cemetery.

In 1980 Southwark Council 'restored' Nunhead Cemetery's West Lodge at a cost of £105,000, but little was done to improve the overall appearance of the cemetery, and local residents and grave owners became increasingly disappointed and concerned at the continuing decline of the cemetery and delays to the Council's plans for the site.

In August 1981, the Scouts' Path, a principal road running through the middle of the cemetery, was widened to provide access for vehicles and heavy machinery. All gravestones on the right hand side of the 'Scouts' Path' leading south from the chapel were removed and broken up, including a pedestal monument commemorating the Victorian music hall entertainer 'The Great Vance' (1840-1888), together with the remains of the Boy Scouts' memorial, an important monument by Sir Giles Gilbert Scott. Regrettably, the life-sized bronze figure of a mourning Scout was stolen in 1969 when Nunhead Cemetery was abandoned by its owners.

Also that summer, practically every brick grave and burial vault on the

Dissenters' Road was broken into: coffins were smashed and human remains desecrated, including those of the eminent Strict Baptist preacher, the Revd James Wells (1803-1872) of the Surrey Tabernacle, Walworth, whose coffin was dragged from its resting place and dashed to pieces. Elsewhere in the cemetery vaults and brick graves continued to be vandalised and broken into, which is not surprising as all the cemetery staff were based at Camberwell New Cemetery and, as a consequence, Nunhead Cemetery was left unattended.

By now local residents had had enough. Jeff Hart, the enthusiastic Vice-Chairman of the Nunhead Residents' Association, was determined to do something about the continuing neglect and vandalism. He convened a meeting of like-minded friends and local councillors, and brought together representatives of the Peckham Society, Southwark Friends of the Earth, the London Wildlife Trust, and several other groups and individuals, who had expressed an interest in the cemetery.

On the 4th November 1981, the Friends of Nunhead Cemetery (FONC), a non party-political voluntary organisation, was inaugurated. Jeff Hart was elected Co-ordinator, Ron Woollacott as Chairman, Chris Knowles as Vice-Chairman, and Chris's wife, Mary Anne Bonney, was elected Secretary.[2]

FONC and Southwark Council

The Friends of Nunhead Cemetery immediately entered into discussions with Southwark Council in an attempt to influence the future development of the cemetery as a nature reserve and local amenity, as well as a place of historic importance and remembrance.

At a specially convened meeting between representatives of FONC and Southwark Council officials, which took place at Southwark Town Hall on the 18th January 1982, Bob Cook of the Borough Engineer's Department, the department responsible for Nunhead Cemetery at that time, maintained that the aspirations of Southwark Council and FONC were the same, although differences were bound to arise in both emphasis and details. He said the 'Friends' were welcome to monitor work undertaken by the Council and to advise on any future plans.[3]

On the 22nd June 1982, at the invitation of FONC, Dr (now Professor Emeritus) James Stevens Curl, a leading authority on Georgian and Victorian architecture, and one of the first academics to draw the general public's attention to the plight of the great commercial cemeteries of the 19th century, gave a fascinating and well-received illustrated lecture entitled 'Nunhead Cemetery in the Context of the Nineteenth Century Cemetery Movement' to an enthusiastic and packed meeting of 'Friends' and their guests.[4]

As a result of the constant pressure exerted by FONC, Southwark Council agreed to set up a Cemetery Working Party made up of elected Councillors from Southwark's Highways and Works Committee, and Libraries and Amenities Committee (the two bodies then responsible for the Burial and Open Space areas). Several officers from a 'bewildering' number of Council departments, and

The Future of
Nunhead Cemetery
& Nunhead Park

Public Meeting 7.30pm. Tuesday,
7th September 1982 at Saint Silas
Church Hall, Inverton Road, S.E.15
Councillors and Officers will be
present to seek your views on
how the appearance of
Nunhead Cemetery and Park
should be improved
Please come along to the meeting
and tell us your views.
Southwark a London borough

Poster announcing a public meeting about the future of Nunhead Cemetery and Park 1982

representatives from an equally bewildering number of voluntary groups, including FONC, the Victorian Society, the Peckham Society, the London Wildlife Trust, the Nunhead Residents' Association, and numerous local tenants' and residents' groups.

Some Councillors were concerned that the local groups represented were not local enough, consequently a special public meeting was held at St Silas's Church Hall, Inverton Road, Nunhead, on the 7th September 1982. The purpose of this meeting was to seek the views of all those residents that resided in the surrounding streets on how the appearance of Nunhead Cemetery/Park should be improved. The meeting was well attended and, from FONC's point of view, a resounding success. When the meeting drew to a close dozens of residents, who were eager to support FONC, hurriedly signed membership forms. Maggie Hart, a founder member remarked that, whilst the Council may not have consulted local people in the past, it had to listen to them now.[5]

FONC organises tours and voluntary work in the cemetery

To encourage interest in the cemetery FONC organised guided tours which proved to be very popular with visitors and continue to be held on a monthly basis to this day.

Workdays were arranged and volunteers set about clearing litter and other rubbish from the cemetery, including burnt-out cars and abandoned furniture. Much work has been carried out by volunteers over the years including minor repairs to monuments; closing brick graves and burial vaults broken into by vandals; removing sycamore growth; pulling Japanese knotweed; keeping paths clear of bramble; and new planting. Other work has included helping people trace family graves to recording monumental inscriptions.

To keep members up to date with events and activities, the first issue of a newsletter was published in 1982. It is now a multi-page magazine of which around 900 copies are printed and distributed to members every quarter.

For the first time in many years, an All Souls Service was held at Nunhead on Sunday 7th November 1982 to remember all those laid to rest in the cemetery. The ecumenical service, organised by FONC members Joan and Alan Bond of St Thomas the Apostle RC Church, Nunhead, in association with St Antony's and St Silas' C of E Churches, Nunhead, was attended by over 70 people. The service is now an annual event.

An early FONC member, Joe Higman, a keen ornithologist, carried out a bird survey in 1982/83. The wren was the most common breeding species with more than 60 pairs holding territories, followed by the blackbird and the robin. Starlings, dunnocks, great and blue tits and song thrushes were numerous, with a few crows and lots of wood pigeons. The wintering fieldfare, redwings and bramblings had left Nunhead Cemetery by the end of March 1983, while the mistle thrushes, redpolls and chaffinches had stayed on in the cemetery till mid-April.

FONC was still in its infancy in 1983, when it was decided to put its workings on a formal basis. A general committee was elected at the first Annual General Meeting in May and the following officers were elected: Ron Woollacott (Chairman); Chris Knowles (Vice-Chairman); Jeff Hart (Co-ordinator); Okell Chee (Treasurer); Mary Anne Bonney (Secretary).

John Collings, Simon Dale, Joe Higman, Diana Ladas, Hilary Wheeler and Maureen Woollacott were elected to serve on the General Committee. Copies of the late Wally Macfarlane's history of the Scottish Political Martyrs, FONC's first major publication, were on sale and, as the group hoped to become a registered charity, a copy of a draft constitution was sent to the Charity Commission for their comments.

The work and activities of FONC gathers momentum

In July 1986, after five years of meetings and negotiations with Southwark Council, FONC was granted a licence to carry out certain tasks within the cemetery, and that summer over 1,000 visitors attended Nunhead Cemetery's first 'Open Day' which was organised by FONC in association with Southwark Council.[6] The Open Day is now an annual event in May, when upwards of 2,000 people come from far and wide to enjoy a pleasant day out in Nunhead's 'countryside'.

On Saturday 9th June 1990, FONC hosted the fourth AGM of the National Federation of Cemetery Friends which brought together ten 'Friends' groups from around the country. The meeting began with a tour of Nunhead Cemetery, and this was followed by a buffet lunch in the Linden Grove Community Hall. The AGM took place in the afternoon, and at FONC's invitation, the meeting was also attended by Professor James Stevens Curl and Jack Maher, President of the Institute of Burial and Cremation Administrators.

On Sunday 29th July 1990, an Ecumenical Service, commemorating the 150th anniversary of the consecration of Nunhead Cemetery, was organised by the Friends of Nunhead Cemetery. The service of celebration was led by the late Right Revd Hugh Montefiore, Assistant Bishop of Southwark, and was attended by, among other dignitaries, Gerald Bowden Conservative MP for Southwark, Dulwich; Simon Hughes, Liberal Democrat MP for Southwark, Bermondsey; and Councillor John Maurice, Worshipful Mayor of Southwark. Harriet Harman, Labour MP for Southwark, Peckham, was invited but was unable to attend. The Nunhead Salvation Army Band provided the music.[7]

In 1991 Cathy Howard, FONC treasurer, started a Sunday afternoon enquiry desk in the cemetery which has proved to be very popular. As well as providing information and advising visitors, FONC publications were on sale including an illustrated guide book and a book listing some notables buried in the cemetery.

New memorial placed on grave of the Walworth Scouts

'The mood of remembrance, hopeful not sombre, characterised the Service of Dedication of the new memorial to the nine Walworth scouts drowned at sea in 1912', wrote John Turpin, FONC's Vice-Chairman, successor to Chris Knowles, about the special service organised by the Friends on Sunday 26th April 1992. The new memorial, in the shape of an open book, replaced the original 'lost' monument by Sir Giles Gilbert Scott. FONC Member Rex Batten was instrumental in obtaining the new memorial which was donated by the funeral directors Francis Chappell & Son and Kellaways. Despite steady rain, over 150 people attended the open-air ecumenical service introduced by Father Robert Browne of St Antony with St Silas. Intercessions were led by Father Geoff Cridland of St Thomas the Apostle RC Church, and the Revd Jed Davis of Peckham Methodist Church, spoke of the significance of the tragedy back in 1912 when the Scout Movement was still very young. Gerald Bowden, former Conservative MP for Dulwich, read from St Mark's Gospel, and Father Tony Davies of St John's Church, Walworth (the parish to which the Scout troop was affiliated) spoke the words of Dedication. The Nunhead Salvation Army Band provided the music, and a young bugler from Dulwich College sounded *The Last Post*.[8]

Rex Batten's book, *The Leysdown Tragedy*, which tells the moving story of the Walworth Scouts, was published in time to make its appearance at that year's Open Day and signed copies were in great demand.

Scottish political martyrs remembered

On a warm summer Sunday in 1993, another major event took place at Nunhead when a solitary Highland piper led a procession of Friends of Nunhead Cemetery, local dignitaries and members of the public, into the cemetery to commemorate the 200th anniversary of the trials of the five 'Scottish Political Martyrs' sentenced to transportation for advocating the principle of universal suffrage. The lofty granite cenotaph, erected to their memory by the radical politician Joseph Hume in 1851, occupies a prominent position in Nunhead Cemetery close to the main entrance.

Among the speakers on that sunny Sunday afternoon were local councillors representing the three major political parties, i.e. Conservative, Labour and Liberal Democrats; Eric Paine of the Thomas Paine Society; Councillor Mrs Cecille Lothian, the Worshipful Mayor of Southwark; and

99

Event at Nunhead Cemetery in 1993 commemorating the 200th anniversary of the trials of the five 'Scottish Political Martyrs'

the late Wally Macfarlane, a local Communist, and early member of FONC and the author of *The Scottish Martyrs*, FONC's first best seller.[9]

FONC leases East Gate Lodge with a view to restoration

In 1994 Southwark Council signed an agreement with FONC allowing the Friends to lease the dilapidated East Gate Lodge in Nunhead Cemetery with a view to its eventual restoration. With financial assistance from English Heritage work on the first phase of preparing the site began almost immediately and, in February 1996 the second phase, including stabilising the building and erecting scaffolding, commenced after a long period of 'bureaucratic' delay. John Collings, an architect and a member of FONC, prepared the schedule of works and the outline layout for the interior of the building, and it was hoped that one day Bunning's Lodge would provide much needed facilities for an interpretation centre and meeting rooms, together with research and exhibition areas.

On Friday 10th November 1995, the Right Hon John Gummer MP, Secretary of State for the Environment, visited Nunhead Cemetery and was greeted by five members of FONC's General Committee. This was a personal visit, without the involvement of Southwark Council, because Mr Gummer wished to see some of the great Victorian cemeteries for himself. He recognised the potential of sites such as Nunhead Cemetery for their historic, ecological and educational importance, and wished to encourage such use. The Secretary of State shared FONC's enthusiasm for carrying out sensitive repairs to the Anglican chapel in order to maintain it as a romantic Gothic ruin while providing safe access to the public.

The seal of the London Cemetery Company is discovered

In August 1997, a rusty old safe which had been languishing in the ruins of the East Gate Lodge for many years, was opened by staff of Southwark Parks Ranger Service. In the absence of keys to the safe, and considering the condition it was in, a decision was made to break it open using a heavy sledge hammer. Inside was a small box containing a collection of rusty old keys, a coffin handle, an old ledger believed to be a record of shareholders of the London Cemetery Company, and another much smaller book. Unfortunately damp and age had destroyed the books beyond legibility.

The most interesting find was the former cemetery company's bronze seal, four centimetres in diameter, with the words: 'London Cemetery Company incor. Anno Dom. 1836' encircling the design of a classical funerary monument bearing the inscription 'sacred to', three female mourning figures, an urn, and the branch of a weeping willow.[10]

Historic core of Nunhead Cemetery 'restored' with lottery grant

In 1998 FONC received HM Queen Elizabeth the Queen Mother's Birthday Award (National Commendation for Environmental Improvements), and the Heritage Lottery Fund (HLF) awarded Nunhead Cemetery £1.25 million under the 'Urban Parks Programme' following a joint application by Southwark Council and FONC. Matched funding came from the Council in the form of four Parks Ranger posts which meant that for the first time in 23 years staff would be on permanent duty in the cemetery. The capital works were concentrated in the 'Heritage Core' of the cemetery, which included the restoration of 50 key monuments; the consolidation of the Anglican chapel; restoration of the main gates, boundary walls and railings; and hard and soft landscaping, including reinstating the view over London looking towards St Paul's Cathedral.[11]

Completion of the restoration works coincided with FONC's Annual Open Day in May 2001, and provided the ideal opportunity to hold a pub-

FONC's Chairman (left) and Councillor Hilary Wines, Mayor of Southwark, accompany the Revd Alan Bond at the official opening of the 'restored' Nunhead Cemetery in May 2001

lic ceremony attended by Councillor Hilary Wines, the Worshipful Mayor of Southwark, and representatives of the various firms involved in the restoration. A long-standing FONC member, the Revd Alan Bond of St Thomas the Apostle RC Church, Nunhead, conducted the ecumenical religious service and a local choir performed in the 'open-air' chapel. An estimated 2,000 visitors enjoyed homemade refreshments and a variety of stalls and exhibitions relating to conservation, natural history, local history, genealogy, and historic cemeteries. Several conducted tours of the cemetery were arranged and visitors were able to enter the 'restored' catacombs beneath the Anglican chapel for the very first time.

Plaque to Walworth Scouts installed in Anglican chapel

A further tribute to the drowned Walworth Scouts *(see page 99)* was held at the Annual Open Day on 17th May 2003, when a replica of the bronze plaque from the original memorial was unveiled in the Anglican chapel by FONC's Rex Batten. The plaque had been stolen in the 1960s but to

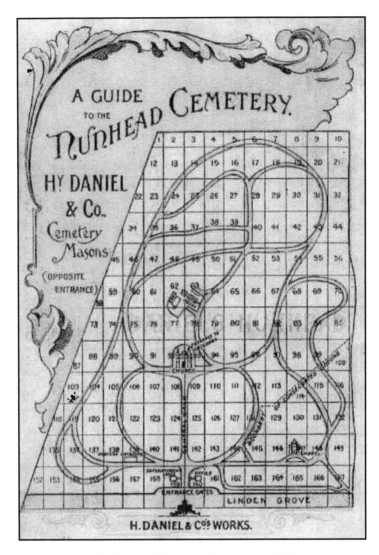

Grid plan of Nunhead Cemetery c.1875

the surprise and delight of FONC, the original plaque was discovered in a scrap yard, and later given to the Scout Association. The dedication service was attended by members of the Filmer and Skipsey families (relatives of three of the Scouts who lost their lives on that fateful day), and led by the Revd Alan Bond of St Thomas the Apostle RC Church and

Father Anthony Braddock-Southgate of St Antony with St Silas. *The Last Post* was sounded by Scout bugler Edward Allberry of Dulwich College.[12]

Postscript

At the time of writing (2010) Nunhead Cemetery is a Grade II* listed landscape and Highgate Cemetery is now listed Grade I.

It was the likes of Professor Emeritus James Stevens Curl and other like-minded persons, who first brought the plight of the magnificent - but sadly neglected - 19th century cemeteries to the notice of the general public back in the 1970s, but it was the perseverance, dedication, enthusiasm and hard work of FONC and FOHC volunteers that helped save the remarkable Victorian cemeteries at Nunhead and Highgate for all to appreciate and enjoy. Both cemeteries are now visited by a much wider public and their future as ecological and historical sites is assured.

APPENDIX:
THE NATIONAL FEDERATION OF
CEMETERY FRIENDS

In 1986, eight 'Friends of Cemeteries' groups got together and formed the National Federation of Cemetery Friends (NFCF). The founding groups were: the Friends of Highgate Cemetery in London, and Friends of Nunhead Cemetery, also in London; the Friends of Undercliffe Cemetery, Bradford, Yorks; the Friends of Beckett Street Cemetery, Leeds, South Yorks; the Friends of the Rosary Cemetery, Norwich; the Friends of York Cemetery; the Friends of Brookwood Cemetery in Surrey; and Save Abney Park Cemetery Campaign. It was felt that with cemeteries increasingly under threat from 'avaricious owners, neglect or ignorance', the NFCF would encourage the conservation of those cemeteries at risk, and promote mutual help and support between cemetery groups. The first annual gathering of delegates was hosted by the Friends of Highgate Cemetery in London.[1]

At the time of writing (2010) the NFCF has around 90 members (groups and individuals).

For further information see the NFCF publication *Saving Cemeteries - a Handbook for Cemetery Friends*, revised edition published in 2009, or check out the NFCF website http://cemeteryfriends.org.uk

NOTES & REFERENCES

1: Historical Background

[1] *The Leisure Hour*, No 231, 29th May 1856, p. 343.

[2] Clare Gittings, *Death, Burial and the Individual in Early Modern England*, London, 1984, pp. 75-6; Ralph Houlbrooke (ed.), *Death, Ritual and Bereavement*, London, 1989, chapter VII, *Why was Death so big in Victorian Britain?* by Ruth Richardson, pp. 109-112. See also Daniel Cohen, *The Body Snatchers*, London, 1977.

[3] George Alfred Walker, *Gatherings from Graveyards,* London, 1839, reprinted New York, 1977, pp. 181-182; *Report from the Select Committee on Improvement of the Health of Towns: Effect of Interment of Bodies in Towns,* 14th June 1842, pp. 48-53; Mrs Basil Holmes, *The London Burial Grounds*, London, 1896, pp. 193-194; Ron Woollacott, *Southwark's Burying Places, Past and Present,* Nunhead, 2001, pp. 14 and 16.

[4] George Alfred Walker, op.cit., pp. 154-158; Charles Knight (ed), *London,* London, 1843, vol 4, pp.163-164.

[5] Edward Walford, *Old and New London,* vol 5, London, 1887, p. 220.

[6] For a history of Kensal Green Cemetery see James Stevens Curl, *The Victorian Celebration of Death,* Newton Abbot, 1972, pp. 54-77; *A Celebration of Death,* London, 1980, pp. 213-223; Paul Coones, *Kensal Green Cemetery: London's First Great Extramural Necropolis*, Ancient Monuments Society Transactions, London, 1987; James Stevens Curl, *The Victorian Celebration of Death,* new edition, Stroud, 2000, pp. 48-68; James Stevens Curl (ed), *Kensal Green Cemetery: The Origins and Development of the General Cemetery of All Souls, Kensal Green, London, 1824-2001,* Chichester, 2001.

[7] *Pigot's Directory,* 1838.

[8] 2 and 3 William IV c.110.

[9] George Collison, *Cemetery Interment*, London, 1840, pp.158-159.

[10] Philippe Aries, *The Hour of Our Death,* 1981, p. 532.

[11] The first common grave excavated at Nunhead Cemetery was grave number 7, square 22, in 1840 for the burial of Charlotte Saunders. Of 199 interments carried out in Nunhead Cemetery between its opening in July 1840 and the end of December 1842, 90 were in 29 common graves. In 1842, the directors of the General Cemetery Company (Kensal Green Cemetery) reserved seven acres specifically for the burial of paupers of seven London parishes.

[12] George Collison, op.cit., p. 160.

[13] Frederic Boase, *Modern English Biography*, London, 1901 (reprinted 1965), vol 3, cols 1145-6; Edward Walford, *Old and New London*, vol 3, London, c.1875, pp. 31-2.

[14] John Claudius Loudon, *On the Laying out, Planting, and Managing of Cemeteries and on the Improvement of Churchyards*, 1843; new edition, with an introduction by James Stevens Curl, Ivelet Books, 1981.

[15] 13 & 14 Victoria c.52. *An Act to make better Provision for the Interment of the Dead in and near the Metropolis*, August 1850.

[16] Walter Thornbury, *Old and New London*, vol 2, London, 1875, p. 278; James Stevens Curl, *Victorian Architecture*, Newton Abbott, 1973, p.71; Howard Colvin, *A Biographical Dictionary of British Architects 1600 - 1840*, 3rd edition, New Haven & London, 1995, p. 396.

[17] 6 & 7 William IV. c.136.

[18] George Collison, op.cit., p. 172.

[19] John Richardson, *Highgate - Its History since the Fifteenth Century*, New Barnet, 1983, p. 162.

[20] John Richardson, op.cit., p. 160 for an illustration of Geary's original plan for a cemetery at Highgate.

[21] Edward Walford, op.cit., p. 406.

[22] John Gay and Felix Barker, *Highgate Cemetery - Victorian Valhalla*, London, 1984, pp. 24-5.

[23] John Richardson, op.cit., p. 162.

[24] *The Penny Magazine of the Society for the Diffusion of Useful Kowledge*, Vol VIII, No 495, 21st December 1839.

[25] George Collison, op.cit., pp. 170-1.

[26] James Stevens Curl, *Victorian Architecture*, Newton Abbot and London, 1990, p. 273; *Egyptomania -The Egyptian Revival: a Recurring Theme in the History of Taste*, Manchester, 1994, p.179; *A Dictionary of Architecture*, Oxford, 1999, p. 107.

2: Nunhead Cemetery

[1] Ron Woollacott, *A Historical Tour of Nunhead and Peckham Rye*, Nunhead, 1995, p. 18.

[2] *Ibid.*, p. 9. Richard Edmonds was laid to rest in the Eastern Catacomb on land compulsorily purchased by the London Cemetery Company and previously owned by him.

[3] Contract between the London Cemetery Company and Henry Ewbank,

merchant, of Denmark Hill, Camberwell, signed and dated 9th March 1840. The land to the west of Nunhead Cemetery was later acquired by the Southwark and Vauxhall Water Company in 1850, and four underground reservoirs were constructed on the site between 1871 and 1875. The Victorian reservoirs were demolished and rebuilt by Thames Water in 1994.

[4] George Collison, op.cit., p. 176.

[5] London Cemetery Company, *Index of Burials, Southern Station, Cemetery of All Saints, Nunhead.*

[6] *Ibid.*

[7] The Eastern Catacomb and adjoining shaft catacomb were surveyed by McDowell and Partners, Consulting Engineers, for and on behalf of Southwark Council in October 1975. For more information see the author's *The Victorian Catacombs at Nunhead*, 2003, and James Stevens Curl, *Nunhead Cemetery, London: A History of the Planning, Architecture, Landscaping and Fortunes of a Great Nineteenth-Century Cemetery,* Transactions of the Ancient Monuments Society, New Series, Volume 22, 1977, p. 53.

[8] The location of the Eastern Catacomb (originally beneath the temporary Episcopalian chapel), and the four shaft catacombs and 14 public vaults, are clearly shown on the original *Plan of the Southern Station, Nun-Head,* signed by J. B. Bunning, architect, of Guilford Street, London, and dated 1841.

[9] Nikolaus Pevsner, *The Buildings of England, London*, Volume 2, Harmondsworth, Middlesex, 1952, p. 82

[10] House of Commons, *Report from the Select Committee on Improvement of the Health of Towns; together with the Minutes of Evidence taken before them, and an Appendix, and Index. Effect of Interment of Bodies in Towns,* 1842.

[11] Early documents give the address of London Cemetery Company's Chief Office as 15 New Bridge Street, near Ludgate Circus, Blackfriars. In 1855 the building was numbered 21 New Bridge Street, and between 1866 and 1949 it was 29 New Bridge Street.

[12] Edward Wedlake Brayley, *A Topographical History of Surrey*, London, 1850, p. 265.

[13] The remains of Catherine Olivia Hutton, aged 47, of Herne Hill, were the first to be deposited in the crypt of the Anglican chapel in 1848. Her body was later transferred to brick grave 1290, square 91.

[14] The remains of Jonathan Crocker, late of Hanover Park, Peckham, were

deposited in the crypt of the Dissenters' chapel in 1854. His remains were removed to the crypt of the Anglican chapel in 1952, and the bomb-damaged Dissenters' chapel was demolished.

[15] *Thirty-seventh Annual Report of the Vestry of the Parish of Camberwell, 1892-93*, London, 1893, Appendix: *Memorandum on Epidemic or Asiatic Cholera, addressed to the Public Health Committee* by J. S. Bristowe, Medical Officer of Health for Camberwell, p. 302.

[16] S. E. Finer, *The Life and Times of Sir Edwin Chadwick*, London, 1952, pp. 412-420.

[17] John Richardson, op.cit., p. 89.

[18] *Ilford Cemetery Scheme 1856: Commission of Sewers Report: Companies Cemeteries*. Abstract showing the various fees and charges made at the principal Metropolitan Cemeteries.

[19] Leaflet issued in 1855 by the London Cemetery Company showing fees and regulations relating to the cemeteries at Nunhead and Highgate.

[20] Fees were reduced for the burial of infants.

[21] William Harnett Blanch, *Ye Parish of Camerwell* (Camberwell), London, 1875, pp. 130-131.

[22] Borough of Camberwell, *11th Annual Report*, 1911. See also, the author's *Camberwell Old Cemetery - London's Forgotten Valhalla,* Nunhead, 2000, pp. 12 and 44, and *Southwark's Burying Places - Past and Present,* Nunhead, 2001, p.6.

[23] *Old Ordnance Survey Map, Brockley, 1868,* notes by Ron Woollacott, Alan Godfrey Maps, Gateshead, 1987.

[24] Ron Woollacott, *Southwark's Burying Places,* unpublished, 1985; *Southwark's Burying Places - Past and Present,* Nunhead, 2001, p. 5.

[25] James Stevens Curl, *Victorian Architecture*, Newton Abbott, 1990, p. 274.

[26] *The Times,* 20th July 1864.

3: The Buxton Affair and the Ups and Downs of Recovery

[1] Buxton's grave-boards are described and illustrated by J. C. Loudon in his book *On the Laying out, Planting, and Managing of Cemeteries and the Improvement of Churchyards,* London, 1843, new edition with an introduction by James Stevens Curl, Redhill, 1981.

[2] Much of the information in this chapter has been taken from the *Minutes of the London Cemetery Company.* See also Professor James Stevens Curl's excellent paper *Nunhead Cemetery, London: A History of the Plan-*

ning, Architecture, Landscaping and Fortunes of a Great Nineteenth-Century Cemetery, Transactions of the Ancient Monument Society , London, New Series, Volume 22, 1977, pp. 41-43.

[3] *Baptist Handbook,* 1903, p. 206.

[4] London Cemetery Company, *Register of Owners of Graves and Vaults, Southern Station, Nunhead.*

[5] See *Friends of Nunhead Cemetery Newsletter No.5,* Summer 1983, article by Ron Woollacott. See also the author's *More Nunhead Notables,* London, 1995, p. 9.

[6] Lewisham Local History Society Transactions 1987-88: *Nunhead Cemetery and Lewisham Burials,* article by Ron Woollacott, p. 41.

[7] A number of suites were let to several concerns including: the Natural Guano Company; the Refuge Assurance Company; Proprietary House and Land Corporation Limited; and Fletcher Bannister JP, architect.

[8] 43 & 44 Victoria Ch.41, *Burial Laws Amendment Act,* 7th September, 1880.

[9] London Cemetery Company, *Register of Vaults, Graves, Etc., Southern Station, Nunhead.*

[10] Brian Parsons, *Committed to the Cleansing Flame: The Development of Cremation in Nineteenth-Century England,* Reading, 2005, p. 138.

[11] London Cemetery Company, *Shareholders' Minute Book;* M. R. Russell Davies, *The Law of Burial, Cremation and Exhumation,* London, 1974, pp. 28-9.

4: A New Century, Renewed Prosperity and Two World Wars

[1] London Cemetery Company, *Register of Owners of Graves and Vaults, Nunhead Cemetery.*

[2] The Waverley Park Estate was laid out by Edward Yates, a speculative builder of Walworth, between 1877 and 1901, and covers the site of four fields comprising about 19 acres to the east and south of Nunhead Cemetery. For a history of the estate see H. J. Dyos, *Victorian Suburb - A Study of the Growth of Camberwell,* Leicester, 1961, pp. 130-137.

[3] The story of the Scouts' tragedy is told by Rex Batten in two publications: *The Leysdown Tragedy - An account of the tragic deaths and spectacular funeral of eight Walworth Scouts drowned at Leysdown in 1912,* Nunhead, 1992; *The Walworth Scouts - An Account of the Leysdown Tragedy of 1912 and Souvenir of the Dedication of the Replica Plaque at Nunhead from the Sir Giles Gilbert Scott Memorial,* Nunhead, 2003

[4] London Cemetery Company, *Register of Owners of Graves and Vaults, Nunhead Cemetery.*

[5] Letter from Mr F. E. Thompson of Harrow to *South London Press* 17th August 1979.

[6] Monuments and gravestones are generally the property of those persons granted the burial rights, and it is their responsibility to keep their graves and memorials in good repair. Some grave owners paid a fee to the London Cemetery Company to maintain their graves in good condition for a limited period or in perpetuity. Headstones were laid face down and larger structures demolished by order of the Board if they were found to be in a poor or dangerous condition.

[7] Information about Mr Gillingham kindly provided by Mr Frank Zobel.

[8] The land for the proposed public cemetery at Honor Oak was acquired by the newly constituted Metropolitan Borough of Camberwell in 1901. Part of the site was laid out as a burial ground and consecrated by the Bishop of Woolwich in 1927 and a section was set aside for members of the Free Churches. The remaining acreage was mapped out into squares and held in reserve for future use. A small piece of the land was taken over for burial purposes in recent years, and the remainder is used as a recreation ground.

[9] Much of the information concerning bomb damage in the cemeteries is based on the notes in the *Register of Owners Graves, Nunhead* and cemetery grid plans for both Highgate and Nunhead Cemeteries; and local knowledge.

[10] George Potter, *Father Potter of Peckham: A South London Saga,* London, 1955, p. 103.

[11] London Cemetery Company Ltd, *Nunhead Cemetery Wages Book.*

[12] M. R. Russell Davies, *The Law of Burial, Cremation and Exhumation,* London, 1974, p.37, note 1; London Cemetery Company Ltd, *Directors Minute Book 1952-9.*

[13] Personal knowledge.

[14] London Cemetery Company Ltd, *Directors' Minute Book 1952-9.*

5: The Demise of the London Cemetery Company and Closure of Nunhead Cemetery

[1] London Cemetery Company Ltd, *Directors' Minute Book 1952-9.*

[2] *Sunday Mirror, 16 August 1970.*

[3] *South London Press, 15th February 1980.*

[4] Unidentified newspaper cutting.

[5] Lucinda Lambton, 'Britain's Vanishing Victoriana' *Observer Magazine*, 22nd October 1972, p. 24; F. A. Wragg, Acting Borough Engineer and Surveyor, Borough of Southwark, *A Condensed History of Nunhead Cemetery*, 1983, p. 5.

[6] London Borough of Southwark, *Nunhead Cemetery: Joint Report by Deputy Town Clerk, Borough Engineer, Borough Treasurer, and Borough Development Officer.* Document HW 3/74-75, 13th June 1974, p. 2.

[7] *Ibid.,* pp. 6-7.

[8] D. Rogers, 'The Wilderness of Nunhead' *Illustrated London News*, December, 1972.

[9] Ron Woollacott, 'Brief Guide to Nunhead Cemetery' *Peckham Society Newsletter 4*, Feb/Mar 1976.

[10] *South London Press,* Tuesday, 30th October 1973; information from the late Dr Frank Rackow, FONC member.

[11] Notes of a meeting about Nunhead Cemetery which took place at the House of Commons, Tuesday 26th March 1974.

[12] *South London Press*, 20th September 1974; Letter to the author about Southwark Council's proposed acquisition of Nunhead Cemetery dated 6th November 1974, signed A. J. Allen, LL.B, AMBIM, Deputy Town Clerk. See also James Stevens Curl, 'Saving a Victorian Burial-Ground. Nunhead Cemetery, South London', *Country Life*, 17th July 1975, pp. 146-8.

[13] *Greater London Council (General Powers) Act 1975, Section 19.*

[14] *South London Press,* 17th October 1975.

[15] Anthony Wragg, Deputy Borough Engineer and Surveyor, London Borough of Southwark, *Nunhead Cemetery: Seminar at North East London Polytechnic*, 13th January 1977.

[16] Southwark Council proposed that the open space area within the cemetery should be called Waverley Park, after the nearby Victorian housing development of the same name. Following local objections it was later decided to use the name Nunhead Park and Cemetery. However, a section of Nunhead Cemetery continues to be shown as Waverley Park on recent maps, including those published by Southwark Council.

[17] Information supplied by Mr F. A. Wragg, Acting Borough Engineer and Surveyor, London Borough of Southwark, April 1983.

[18] A society called the 'Friends of Highgate Cemetery' held its preliminary meeting on 17th June 1975, and was inaugurated on 9th October 1975. The Acting Secretary was Mrs J. A. Pateman MBE, who later

served as Chairman until 2009.

[19] John Gay & Felix Barker, op.cit., p. 20.

[20] Friends of Highgate Cemetery Limited, *Annual Review, 2000/2001.*

6: Nunhead's New Friends

[1] *South London Press, 26 October 1979.*

[2] *Minutes of the inaugural meeting of the Friends of Nunhead Cemetery,* 4th November 1981.

[3] Notes on a meeting between representatives of the Friends of Nunhead Cemetery and officers of Southwark Borough Council, held at 10am on Monday 18th January 1982 at Southwark Town Hall. Those present were Bob Cook and Ian Williams of the Borough Engineer's Department, and Philip Collins of Southwark Council's Landscape Architect's Department. Jeff Hart and Chris Knowles attended on behalf of FONC.

[4] *Friends of Nunhead Cemetery Newsletter* No 1, Summer 1982.

[5] *Friends of Nunhead Cemetery Newsletter* No 2, Autumn 1982.

[6] London Borough of Southwark, *Southwark Sparrow,* September 1986, p. 13.

[7] *Friends of Nunhead Cemetery Newsletter* No. 32, Summer/Autumn 1990.

[8] John Turpin, 'Scouts Memorial Dedicated' *Friends of Nunhead Cemetery Newsletter* No. 38, p. 2, June 1992; Rex Batten, *The Walworth Scouts,* Nunhead, 2003, pp. 20-21.

[9] John Clough, 'Sun Shines on Scottish Martyrs Event' *Friends of Nunhead Cemetery Newsletter* No. 44, pp. 4 -5, December 1993.

[10] *Friends of Nunhead Cemetery Newsletter No 58,* September 1997

[11] Scott Wilson, *The Restoration of Nunhead Cemetery - Fact Sheet,* 2001.

[12] Rex Batten, 'The Dedication of the Scout Memorial Plaque' *FONC News* New Series No 5 (issue No 81), pp. 11-12, Autumn, September - November 2003.

Appendix: The National Federation of Cemetery Friends

[1] *The Friends of Nunhead Cemetery Newsletter No 18,* Autumn 1986.

SOURCES & FURTHER READING

Commission of Sewers Report: *Ilford Cemetery Scheme 1856: Companies Cemeteries*. Abstract showing the various fees and charges made at the principal Metropolitan Cemeteries.

Greater London Council: *Greater London Council General Powers Act 1975, Section 19*.

House of Commons: *Report from the Select Committee on Improvement of the Health of Towns; together with the Minutes of Evidence taken before them, and an Appendix, and Index. Effect of Interment of Bodies in Towns*, 1842.

London Borough of Southwark, *Nunhead Cemetery: Joint Report by Deputy Town Clerk, Borough Engineer, Borough Treasurer, and Borough Development Officer*. Document HW 3/74-75, 13th June 1974.

London Cemetery Company, *Leaflet issued in 1855 showing fees and regulations*.

London Cemetery Company, *Shareholders' Minute Book 1863-1959*.

London Cemetery Company, *Index of Burials, Southern Station, Cemetery of All Saints, Nunhead*.

London Cemetery Company, *Register of Owners of Graves and Vaults, Southern Station, Nunhead*.

London Cemetery Company, *Nunhead Day Books*, various years.

London Cemetery Company, *The Rules, Orders and Regulations of the London Cemetery Company, made pursuant to 6 & 7 William 4th, cap cxxxvi, and 6 Victoria, cap xxxvi. For the Management and Regulation of their Cemeteries, and of the Catacombs, Vaults, Graves, and Monuments therein*. May 6th, 1902.

London Cemetery Company Ltd, *Incumbents Fees, Nunhead, 1933-43*.

London Cemetery Company Ltd, *Directors Minute Book 1952-9*.

McDowell & Partners, *Victorian Catacombs, Nunhead Cemetery, Southwark, Building Surveys and Structural Report*, 1976.

Anthony Wragg, Deputy Borough Engineer and Surveyor, London Borough of Southwark, *Nunhead Cemetery: Seminar at North East London Polytechnic*, 13th January 1977.

Catharine Arnold, *Necropolis - London and Its Dead*, Simon & Schuster, 2006.

Sylvia Barnard, *Notes on Saving Cemeteries,* National Federation of

Cemetery Friends, 1988.

Rex Batten, *The Leysdown Tragedy - An Account of the Deaths and Funeral of Eight Walworth Scouts in 1912*, Friends of Nunhead Cemetery (FONC), 1992.

Rex Batten (ed), *Nunhead Remembered - A Collection of Stories, Anecdotes and Observations from Nunhead Cemetery*, FONC, 1995.

Rex Batten, *Nunhead and the Music Hall - An Account of the Music Hall Personalities buried in Nunhead Cemetery*, FONC, 2000.

Rex Batten, *The Walworth Scouts - An Account of the Leysdown Tragedy of 1912 and Souvenir of the Dedication of the Replica Plaque at Nunhead from the Sir Giles Gilbert Scott Memorial*, FONC, 2003.

Darren Beach, *London Cemeteries*, Metro Publications, 2006.

Chris Brooks et al, *Mortal Remains -The History and Present State of the Victorian and Edwardian Cemetery*, Wheaton, 1989.

George Collison, *Cemetery Interment*, Longman, Orme, Brown, Green and Longmans, 1840.

James Stevens Curl, *The Victorian Celebration of Death*, David & Charles, 1972; new edition, Sutton Publishing, 2000.

James Stevens Curl, *Nunhead Cemetery, London*, Transactions of the Ancient Monuments Society, New Series, Volume 22, 1977.

James Stevens Curl, *A Celebration of Death, - An Introduction to some of the Buildings, Monuments, and Settings of Funerary Architecture in the Western European Tradition*, Constable, 1980.

James Stevens Curl, *Victorian Architecture*, David & Charles, 1990.

James Stevens Curl, *Egyptomania -The Egyptian Revival: a Recurring Theme in the History of Taste*, Manchester University Press, 1994.

James Stevens Curl (ed), *Kensal Green Cemetery - The Origins and Development of the General Cemetery of All Souls, Kensal Green, London, 1824-2001*, Phillimore, 2001.

James Stevens Curl, *Death and Architecture - An Introduction to Funerary and Commemorative Buildings in the Western European Tradition, with Some Consideration of their Settings*, Sutton Publishing, 2002.

Brent Ellott et al, *Highgate Cemetery*, Friends of Highgate Cemetery, 1978.

Mauro Felicori and Annalisa Zanotti (eds), *A Guidebook to Cemeteries of Europe - A Historical Heritage to Appreciate and Restore*, Association of Significant Cemeteries in Europe, 2004.

John Gay and Felix Barker, *Highgate Cemetery - Victorian Valhalla*, John Murray, 1984.

Historic Buildings and Monuments Commission, *Register of Parks and Gardens of Special Historic Interest in England, part 17, Greater London,* English Heritage, 1988.

Mrs Basil (Isabel) Holmes, *The London Burial Grounds,* Fisher and Unwin, 1896.

Richard A. Jones, *The Butterflies of Nunhead Cemetery,* FONC, 1997.

Charles Knight (ed), *London,* Volume IV, Chapter LXXXVI, London. Burials by J. Saunders, 1843.

John Claudius Loudon, *On the Laying out, Planting, and Managing of Cemeteries and on the Improvement of Churchyards,* 1843; new edition, with an introduction by James Stevens Curl, Ivelet Books, 1981.

Wally Macfarlane, *The Scottish Martyrs - The Story of the Political Reformers of 1793-4,* FONC, 1983.

Hugh Meller, *London Cemeteries: An Illustrated Guide and Gazetteer,* Avebury Publishing, 1981.

Hugh Meller and Brian Parsons, *London Cemeteries: An Illustrated Guide and Gazetteer,* fourth edition, History Press, 2008.

John Morley, *Death, Heaven and the Victorians,* Studio Vista, 1971.

NFCF, *Saving Cemeteries - A Handbook for Cemetery Friends,* National Federation of Cemetery Friends, 2009.

Brian Parsons, *The London Way of Death,* Sutton Publishing, 2001.

Brian Parsons, *Committed to the Cleansing Flame - The Development of Cremation in Nineteenth-Century England,* Spire Books Ltd, 2005.

Ruth Richardson, *Death, Dissection and the Destitute,* Routledge and Kegan Paul, 1987.

Bob Smyth, *City Wildspace,* Hilary Shipman, 1987.

Bob Smyth, *The Green Guide to Urban Wildlife,* A & C Black, 1990.

Carol Stevenson, *Trees and Shrubs of Nunhead Cemetery,* FONC, 1998.

Tim and Carol Stevenson (editors), *A Short Guide to Nunhead Cemetery,* FONC, 2003, reprinted 2006.

Gwyneth Stokes (ed), *Illustrated Guide to Nunhead Cemetery,* FONC, 1988; revised edition 1995.

George Alfred Walker, *Gatherings from Grave Yards, Particularly those of London,* Longman & Co, 1839, reprinted Arno Press, USA, 1977.

Jenifer White and Joan Hodsdon (eds), *Paradise Preserved - An Introduction to the Assessment, Evaluation, Conservation and Management of Historic Cemeteries,* English Heritage, 2007.

Ron Woollacott, *Investors in Death - A History of the London Cemetery Company and its Successors,* unpublished manuscripts 1977 to date.

Ron Woollacott, *Nunhead Notables - Some of the Interesting and Important Men and Women buried in London's Nunhead Cemetery,* FONC, 1984, reprinted with plan 1987.
Ron Woollacott, *A Guide to the Graves of Nunhead Notables,* FONC, 1986.
Ron Woollacott, *More Nunhead Notables,* FONC, 1995.
Ron Woollacott, *Camberwell Old Cemetery - London's Forgotten Valhalla,* Maureen and Ron Woollacott, 2000.
Ron Woollacott, *Southwark's Burying Places, Past & Present - A Guide to Burial Grounds in the London Borough of Southwark,* Maureen and Ron Woollacott, 2001.
Ron Woollacott, *Nunhead Notables - A Biographical List of Notable Men and Women buried in London's Nunhead Cemetery of All Saints,* FONC, 2002.
Ron Woollacott, *The Victorian Catacombs at Nunhead - A Short History and Description of the Chapel Catacombs, Shaft Catacombs and Eastern Catacomb in Nunhead Cemetery, Southwark,* Maureen and Ron Woollacott, 2003, 2nd edition FONC, 2006.
F. A. Wragg, *A Condensed History of Nunhead Cemetery,* Deputy Borough Engineer and Surveyor, London Borough of Southwark, 1983.

A group of tombs in the Dissenters' ground at Nunhead Cemetery

INDEX
Page numbers in bold italic refer to illustrations

29, 40, 49, 50, 53, 63, 74, 78, 95
Dodd, Henry Martyn 59, 65, 68
Donkin FRS, Bryan 18, 49
Donkin, Bryan 18, 48, 49, 52
Donkin, John 19, 49
Donkin & Co, Ltd, Bryan 49
Doulton of Lambeth 60
Drew MA FRGS, Revd George Smith
   45
Drew, Mrs Mary 45
Duchy of Cornwall 76
Duggan, Louisa 62
Dulwich 17, 41, 98, 99
Dulwich College 99, 104
Durnford, William George 41

Edgington, Benjamin 16
Edinburgh and Leith Cemetery Co Ltd
   83
Edmonds, Richard 23
Egyptian Society of Cairo 42
English Heritage 100
Enon Chapel 12, 13,14
Ewbank, Henry 23

Fenn, Thomas Britten 39
Financial Times 82
Fines, Alexander 82
Floral decoration of graves
   see Flowering Business
Flowering Business 34, 46, 59, 60, 63
Flying bombs (V1s) 75
Forster, Robert 61
Fowler, Joseph Gurney 68
Friends of the Earth 95
Friends of the Rosary Cemetery,
   Norwich 104
Friends of Beckett Street Cemetery,
   Leeds 104
Friends of Brookwood Cemetery,
   Surrey 104
Friends of Highgate Cemetery,
   (FOHC), 93, 104

Friends of Nunhead Cemetery
   (FONC) 94, 95, 98, 99, 104
Friends of Undercliffe Cemetery 104
Friends of York Cemetery 104
Funeral Directors *see* Undertakers

Geary, Stephen 15, 19, 22
General Board of Health 15, 31, 34
General Cemetery Company 12, 13,
   16, 18, 44, 53, 54
General Cemetery Company Act 1832
   13
George IV, Statue of 15
Gibbs, Mr 43
Giffard PC, QC, Sir George Markham
   51
Giffard RN, Admiral John 51
Giffard, Captain James Combes 18,
   44, 49, 50, 51, 52
Giffard, Captain, grave of *52*
Gillingham, George Henry 68, *68*, 74
Glazier, John 53
Golders Green Crematorium 58
Gomm, Field Marshall Sir William 93
Gravediggers 27, 67, *73,* 76, 78
Graves repurchased and resold 44, 45,
   62
Gray DL, JP, Robert Alexander 35
Gray, Revd Percy 86, 89
Greater London Council 87, 88
Greater London Council
   (General Powers) Bill 1975 90, 93
Green, Samuel 62, 63
Greenhouses 46, 59, 67, 81
Gregory, Hugh Graham 77, 79
Gully, Ross, Stephens and Gregory 79
Gummer MP, John 100

Hardwick, Philip Charles 41
Harman MP, Harriet 98
Harris mausoleum at Nunhead 74
Harris, Major William Barclay 75, 76,
   77, 82

119

Pinemarsh Ltd 93
Pole, George 68
Poor, Burial of the 14, 27, 34, 35
Potter, Revd Canon George Potter 75
Preston, David Cripps, 16, 27
Price, Frank Steane 18, 76
Price, Waterhouse and Company 18, 61, 68, 76
Proprietors 16, 17, 18, 31, 38, 39, 42, 43, 46, 51, 53, 56, 65 - *see also shareholders*
Public monuments 34

Queen Elizabeth the Queen Mother's Birthday Award 101

Radlett, Herts 61
Radley's Hotel 17, 38, 39, 40
Raggett, George Louis Edward 69
Ramsay, David 19
Rawlins, Mr 77
Raybar Holdings Ltd 83, 84
Raybar Properties Ltd 83
Raybourne Group Ltd 84, 87, 88, 89, 93
Read, Miss Lillie 66
Register of Shareholders 39, 40
Rosebank Cemetery 83
Rotherhithe 47, 62, 93
Rothesay, Isle of Bute 52
Rouet, Miss Jessie 68
Royal Garrison Artillery 70
Royal Humane Society 36
Russell, Revd Dr John 18, 24, 27, 36, 37, 72
Rutland Lodge, Brixton 49

Salisbury Hotel 17, 43
Scott, Sir Giles Gilbert 66, 94, 99
Scottish Political Martyrs, The 30, 98, 99
Select Committee on the 'Effect of Interment of Bodies in Towns' 27

Shand, Ann Sophia 24
Shand, George Long 24, 25
Shand, Georgiana 24
Shard Estate, The 23
Shareholders 16, 17, 36, 39,40, 41, 49, 52, 53, 54, 56, 57, 58, 59, 60, 62, 63, 64, 65, 67, 68, 69, 70, 71, 74, 76, 77, 78, 82, 101
Shoreham, Kent 23
Simpson, Frederic 49
Simpson, Thomas Bridge 43, 46, 47, 48, 49
Simpson, Thomas Bridge, tomb of *48*
Sir Walter St John's Charity Trust 35
Smallfield, Rawlins and Company 17, 77, 78, 82
Smith, Mrs Margaret 37
Society for the Abolition of Burials 14
Society for the Propagation of the Gospel 37
South London Press 94
South Metropolitan Cemetery Company 24, 66
Southwark, Bishop of 87, 98
Southwark and Vauxhall Water Company 30
Southwark Council, Conservation Areas Advisory Council 92
Southwark Council, Parks Ranger Service 101
Southwark, London Borough of (council) 83, 85, 87, 88. 89, 90, 91,92, 93, 94, 95, 96, 98. 100, 101
Soviet Consulate 82
St Antony with Silas Church, Nunhead 97, 99, 104
St Bride's Institute 17, 77
St Christopher-le-Stocks, City of London 25, 41, 72
St George the Martyr, Southwark, Parish of 36
St Giles, Camberwell, Parish of 23

The Friends of Nunhead Cemetery (FONC)

Registered Charity No 296413
Recipient of HM Queen Elizabeth the Queen Mother's
Birthday Award for Environmental Improvements
(National Commendation) 1998.

FONC is a founder member of the National Federation of Cemetery Friends (NFCF) and a member of the Association of Significant Cemeteries in Europe (ASCE).

FONC was established in 1981 to promote the conservation and appreciation of Nunhead Cemetery as a place of remembrance, historic importance and natural beauty. Members receive a free copy of FONC News, a quarterly journal, containing details of walks and presentations and forthcoming events, as well as feature articles and up-to-date information about the cemetery. Occasional talks and guided visits to other historic cemeteries are arranged, and there's the opportunity to carry out certain conservation work in the cemetery on our popular monthly voluntary workdays. For further information about joining FONC and becoming a member and the current annual subscription rates, please write to the Membership Secretary, Simon Mercer, c/o 31 Normanby Road, LONDON, NW10 1BU or see our website **www.fonc.org.uk**

Free guided tours of the cemetery take place on the last Sunday of every month starting at 2.15pm. Meet at the flint circle inside the main gates. Tours take around 2 hours, though rather less during the winter months.

Nunhead Cemetery is now open to the public from 9.am to 4.00pm daily, and stays open later during the summer months. *Please note that all times are subject to change.* The cemetery may be closed without prior notice for health and safety reasons, for example danger of injury to visitors during very windy and stormy weather. If in any doubt, or before setting out on a long journey, please contact the cemetery staff on 020 7732 9535 for the latest information.

The cemetery is owned by the London Borough of Southwark and is run jointly by Southwark's ranger gardeners and FONC volunteers. For further information see FONC's excellent website **www.fonc.org.uk**

FONC Publications

Please note some of the publications listed below are now out-of-print and no longer available.

The Scottish Martyrs by Wally Macfarlane, 1983, reprinted 1991.
Nunhead Notables by Ron Woollacott, 1984, reprinted with plan 1987 (out of print).
A Guide to the Graves of Nunhead Notables by Ron Woollacott, 1986 (out of print).
Nunhead Cemetery - An Illustrated Guide edited by Gwyneth Stokes, 1987, revised edition 1995 (out of print).
The Leysdown Tragedy by Rex Batten, 1992 (out of print).
More Nunhead Notables by Ron Woollacott, 1995.
Nunhead Remembered by Rex Batten, 1995.
The Butterflies of Nunhead Cemetery by Richard A. Jones, 1997.
Trees and Shrubs of Nunhead Cemetery by Carol Stevenson, 1998.
Nunhead and the Music Hall by Rex Batten, 2000.
Nunhead Notables by Ron Woollacott, revised and expanded edition, 2002.
The Walworth Scouts by Rex Batten, 2003.
A Short Guide to Nunhead Cemetery edited by Tim and Carol Stevenson, 2003, reprinted 2006.
The Victorian Catacombs at Nunhead by Ron Woollacott, 2003, FONC edition 2006.
Nunhead Cemetery - A Colourful History by Fay Rogers and Cathy Mercer, 2009.

Further information about FONC publications and current prices will be found at **www.fonc.org.uk**

Publications are usually on sale at FONC's Portakabin, opposite the Scottish Martyrs' Monument (just inside the main gates in Linden Grove) on the first and last Sunday of each month between 2.00pm and 4.00pm, unless prevented by bad weather conditions or lack of volunteers.